Contending Perspectives in Economics

Contending Perspectives in Economics

A Guide to Contemporary Schools of Thought

John T. Harvey

Texas Christian University, USA

Cheltenham, UK • Northampton, MA, USA

Published by
Edward Elgar Publishing Limited
The Lypiatts
15 Lansdown Road
Cheltenham
Glos GL50 2JA
UK

Edward Elgar Publishing, Inc.
William Pratt House
9 Dewey Court
Northampton
Massachusetts 01060
USA

Paperback edition 2016

A catalogue record for this book
is available from the British Library

Library of Congress Control Number: 2014950752

ISBN 978 0 85793 203 7 (cased)
ISBN 978 0 85793 204 4 (eBook)
ISBN 978 1 78471 948 7 (paperback)

Typeset by Columns Design XML Ltd, Reading
Printed and bound in Great Britain by TJ International Ltd, Padstow

Contents

Acknowledgments

I had more help than usual in writing this volume and owe a great many thanks. It is appropriate that I start with my wife, Melanie, who has not only been enthusiastic about this project since it started, but she also read several chapters and suggested revisions. Both of my daughters, Meg and Alex, did the same, as did one of their friends, Duncan Griffin. Another of their classmates, Max Brozynski, provided research assistance. My students at Texas Christian University (TCU) also helped as they were assigned draft chapters as I wrote them and were therefore able to give feedback. I would also like to thank the university, college, and my department and all my colleagues therein. They are truly supportive and I am lucky to work there.

But that is not all. Because of the nature of this volume, I thought it vital to have each of the heterodox chapters reviewed by one or more members of that particular school of thought. This was very important to me as I wanted to make sure that everyone thought they were treated fairly. Their help was invaluable and, to the best of my knowledge, I incorporated every single criticism and comment save one (see below).

Proceeding in the order that those schools of thought are introduced, Andrew Kliman (Pace University) was of tremendous help in revising the Marxism chapter. He not only told me what I had done wrong, he provided specific references for use in my corrections. Sam Bostaph (University of Dallas), the first person to give me a job interview when I was coming out of graduate school, took time from his retirement to help me improve the Austrian economics chapter. My own colleague here at TCU, Doug Butler, also offered his insights on that chapter and he helped me with my explanation of how economic science really works in Chapter 2. It should be noted that he did this just days after the birth of his first child! Pavlina Tcherneva's (Bard College and the Levy Economics Institute) excellent critique of the chapter on Post Keynesianism caused me to undertake a significant refocus of the discussion of their policy recommendations and to clarify several important issues that I had earlier skimmed over. Paul Dale Bush (California State University at Fresno) read and commented on the Institutionalism chapter and was especially helpful in getting me to rethink the link between that school of thought and Post Keynesianism. Fellow board game geek and TCU economics colleague, Stephen Quinn, gave me comments on the New Institutionalist chapter. One of his was the only recommendation I ignored: he asked that I remove his research from the discussion on the grounds that he is not a "big name." Unfortunately for him, the article in question served to very nicely illustrate a point! Finally, Gillian Hewitson (University of Sydney) and Janice Peterson (California State University at Fresno) gently but firmly corrected my many missteps in the Feminist economics chapter. I am very grateful for their commentary and the many sources they provided.

At Edward Elgar Publishing, my editor, Matthew Pitman, deserves my thanks. I absolutely hate missing deadlines, but I did. Matt understood and continued to support my efforts and trust my instincts. I want to thank Edward Elgar too. I stopped by his booth at the Allied Social Sciences Meetings in Atlanta in 2010, with the sole intention of seeing if he already had a book on this topic. Somehow, after speaking with Edward for about 15 minutes, I walked away having agreed to write one! I am forever grateful, for this has been one of the most rewarding projects of my professional career.

Finally, to all my buddies at the various Starbucks where I wrote so much of this book – Eugene, Neal, Brian, Steph, Scott, Jennifer, Todd, Slavin, Kent, and Slobodan – thanks for your interest, enthusiasm, and friendship!

As always, while I am extremely grateful for the help of all the above individuals, any remaining errors are my own.

1. Introduction

Those who speak only a single language have a necessarily limited view of how humans communicate. They know just one means of constructing a sentence, one manner of changing tense, one word for "table," and so on. If that language is English, they will not realize that others attach genders to nouns, have complex honorific variants, or use tones to infer meaning. They cannot possibly understand what is unique about their own language because they do not know anyone else's.

More than that, language affects how we think. Whether or not one's native tongue has a word for a specific thing or action can impact the individual's perception of it. And learning a second language can enhance your reasoning skills. According to Therese Sullivan Caccavale, President of the National Network for Early Language Learning:

> Additionally, foreign language learning is much more a cognitive problem solving activity than a linguistic activity, overall. [Studies have shown repeatedly that foreign language learning increases critical thinking skills, creativity, and flexibility of mind in young children] Students who are learning a foreign language out-score their non-foreign language learning peers in the verbal and, surprisingly to some, the math sections of standardized tests. (Duke University 2007)

An American who learns French need never travel to France to benefit. The effect on the brain is independent of how one uses the newfound knowledge.

The very same thing is true of learning more than a single school of thought. Institutionalism and Austrianism, for example, approach economics from very different angles, with the former seeing behavior as almost completely social and the latter seeing it as almost completely individualistic. In comparing these, one is forced to tease out the many otherwise unstated and unconscious – yet critical – assumptions being made by both. Their vocabularies are different, their tools of analysis are different, their views of human nature are different, and so on. It is intellectually challenging and liberating to see how another group of scholars views economic behavior. Nor does one have to be an Institutionalist or an Austrian for this exercise to be useful.

1

Unfortunately, the overwhelming majority of economics programs teach only one school of thought or, at best, minor variations thereof. Monetarism and Keynesianism, for example, are both part of Neo-classicism and while comparing them is not without benefit, it is the equivalent of comparing Australian and American English. Knowing only one approach puts blinders on the economist. They say that to a person with a hammer, every problem looks like a nail. Likewise, Post Keynes-ians tend to focus on issues of financial instability, Marxists on the internal contradictions of capitalism, Neoclassicals on maximization under constraints, and so on. Someone familiar with all three, however, is like a person with multiple tools. This is not to suggest that an economist can believe every school of thought is correct. Of course not, for they contain mutually exclusive propositions. Rather, the idea is that the intellectual challenge of comparing divergent approaches means that, even as someone who completely embraces New Institutionalism, aware-ness of how another perspective might examine the same issue makes you much more sensitive to the strengths and weaknesses of your own approach. If you start and finish this book as a Neoclassical, you will still be a better economist because you will have developed a much better *focusing on the determination of goods, outputs, and income distributions in markets through Supply & Demand.* understanding of what Neoclassicism is.

This is why a growing number of economists, associated with the economic pluralism movement, believe that it is vital that we open up our classrooms to more schools of thought. They argue this not only for the pedagogic reasons suggested above but also because it is not apparent that the explanatory power of the dominant approach is actually superior to the others. The Financial Crisis and ensuing Great Recession have certainly contributed to this sentiment.

I was fortunate enough to serve for six years as the director of the International Confederation of Associations for Pluralism in Economics (ICAPE), an organization devoted to providing a forum for debate across paradigms. Although I was already familiar with a variety of schools of thought, my work in ICAPE allowed me to actually meet many of the individuals associated with them and to see the activities they organized. This book is not about the history of economics, but about those people. Everything in here covers a living, breathing school of thought, run by individuals that I would call bright, ambitious, and hard-working – even when I disagree with them!

The goal of this book is not to offer a comprehensive treatment of every school of thought. That would be impossible in a single volume. Rather, my hope is that the student comes away with a solid feel for each approach, an idea of what makes it unique, and sufficient background to delve into the relevant literature in a more informed manner. For that reason, I am quite sure that I have not covered all the topics that every reader might think relevant. If I have omitted something the instructor would have liked to have seen covered, then I encourage her to supplement the book with outside readings. I, however, wanted to keep the volume relatively simple. Another of my concerns was that the student emerges from the course with a new enthusiasm for our discipline. It has been suggested that teaching students more than one school of thought can confuse and demoralize them (Siegfried and Meszaros 1997). Surveys I conducted of my students, however, showed just the opposite (Harvey 2011). Controversy is exciting and it stimulates thinking rather than suppresses it. Controversy is just what you will find here.

Something I discovered when submitting the first chapters of this volume to Edward Elgar Publishing for review was the following: this is a topic about which people are very opinionated and those opinions vary widely. In my case, the very same passages one reviewer praised, the other absolutely hated! Such is the nature of this topic. Given this, I ask the reader's indulgence in working her way through this volume. I did my very best to focus on characteristics that were sufficiently general to be thought common to all members of each particular school of thought. But I know that this is ultimately impossible. In the end, I used my best judgement while trying to focus on the things that were the most unique or interesting in each paradigm.

This book covers seven approaches: Neoclassical, Marxist, Austrian, Post Keynesian, Institutionalist, New Institutionalist, and Feminist. The amount of space devoted to each is not equal because some required more explanation than others. However, every chapter has the same structure so that a common set of issues is addressed. Each starts with a basic description. This is the section that varies most from chapter to chapter because the coverage is dictated by the nature of that school of thought. Some require considerable history, some extra background on specific theories, and so on. After that, the method of analysis preferred by those economists is explained. How do they do research and what do they respect as supporting evidence? Do they use experiments, build computer models, or examine historical trends? In addition, because economics is ultimately the study of people, each chapter also outlines that school of thought's view of human nature. And if economics is policy-oriented, then each approach must have some sense of justice in mind. This, too, is covered.

The next section in each chapter is a description of the primary and secondary standards of behavior enforced by that approach. This is a rather involved concept and a complete explanation must wait until the next chapter, but the basic idea is that Neoclassical economists, for example, must undertake particular activities in a specific manner to gain status in their group. That which makes people say something like "Pat is a great economist!" varies by school of thought. Is it superior teaching, best-selling text books, conference presentations, journal publications, research focused on a particular area or using a specific method, and so on? The answer to that question is neither always obvious nor necessarily associated with doing things that enhance our understanding of the economy. The underlying premise here is that humans are tribal and want to be considered upstanding members of their social group. Economists are no different.

Following this, the contemporary activities of that group are outlined. Do they have an annual meeting, is there a journal where their research is published, and so on? Up to this point of each chapter, my goal will have been to convince the reader that the school of thought in question is the greatest intellectual contribution since the Law of Gravity. I want to portray each perspective the same way a proponent would and thereby not play favorites (even though I clearly have an opinion too). However, every approach must have its detractors too, otherwise we would all believe the same thing. For that reason, an important part of each chapter is the second-to-last section: Criticisms. This describes several common attacks that have been made on the approach in question. This may cause the student some distress if up to that point she had been thoroughly convinced by the arguments in that chapter. But that is okay! Learning is not moving from one point of confidence to another. Doubt is healthy in scholarship because it forces us to search for supporting evidence rather than simply blindly accept. Every school of thought gets a chance to fire back, however, in a Final rejoinder section. Suggestions for further reading finish off every chapter.

One issue that authors of books like this must address is whether or not to mention which schools of thought they follow. My opinion is that the reader deserves to know. While I have tried my very best to be completely unbiased – to the point that I had members of each heterodox school of thought review their chapter to make sure my representation is fair – no one can be absolutely successful in this endeavor. Still, you may want to read this book without knowing how I feel, so I will save that information until the very end. If you want to know now, turn to the last paragraph in the last chapter. Otherwise, read on!

One last thought before starting the business at hand. I remember taking a class in political thought when I was an undergraduate. As we covered each philosopher, for example, Jeremy Bentham, I remember thinking, "Wow, this guy was a genius! I'm following him!" Then we would cover the next political theorist, who had rejected the previous one. "Oh yeah," I found myself saying time after time, "Now that I think about it, that other guy had it all wrong. But this new guy is a genius!" This happened three or four times until I had an epiphany: I don't know what the hell I'm talking about. I am a college sophomore in an introductory-level political science class and the idea that I am going to discern from a few hundred pages of reading and some lectures which political thinker of the past 300 years was best is ludicrous.

I say this not to insult the reader's analytical abilities. Your professors are still struggling to decide what they think is right too. But that realization on my part all those years ago was terribly liberating. It freed me from thinking that my goal was to pick a side and defend it. Instead, it let me sit back and relax and just listen to what everyone had to say. I never had to decide that one person was 100 percent right – and, indeed, no one is – and I could take my time to digest all the perspectives. I could try each one and see how it illuminated, or did not, specific political issues. I cannot tell you what a difference that made to my approach and understanding. I hope you are able to view this book the same way. You never have to decide whether you are an Austrian, a Marxist, or a Feminist. Just relax and see what you learn. But whatever you decide, I challenge you to read this book and not come away thinking the very same thing I do: there is something unique, insightful, and worthwhile in every school of thought.

REFERENCES

Duke University (2007), "The Duke University talent identification program online newsletter for parents of gifted youth," *Duke Gifted Letter*, **8** (1), available at http://www.actfl.org/advocacy/discover-languages/for-parents/cognitive (accessed September 27, 2013).

Harvey, J.T. (2011), "Student attitudes toward economic pluralism: survey-based evidence," *International Journal of Pluralism and Economics Education*, **2** (3), 270–90.

Siegfried, J.J. and B.T. Meszaros (1997), "National voluntary content standards for pre-college economics education," *American Economic Review*, **82** (2), 247–53.

2.   Economics as a scientific discipline

Marxists, Austrians, Neoclassicals, Feminists – these are all subgroups of the larger group called economists. Before trying to understand the elements unique to each individual school of thought, it is necessary to take a step back and look at some of the broader issues that affect them all. To that end, this chapter discusses the nature of scientific inquiry, the means by which we train economists, the reward structure that exists in our profession, and the process by which accepted theory evolves. This detailed outline of the current state of our discipline will create a context within which each school of thought can be understood. A key conclusion of the chapter is that the development of reliable explanations of economic phenomena requires a pluralistic approach to the development of theory, one in which schools of thought debate openly and vigorously in an atmosphere of mutual respect. Unfortunately, the actual structure of our discipline encourages just the opposite.

WHAT IS SCIENCE?

Let us start with a very basic question about which many volumes have been written: what is science? We are taught in primary and secondary school that it is methodical, experimental, and objective and that the world it studies has particular innate characteristics. The job of the scientist is to make careful, unbiased observations and use these to formulate hypotheses. These hypotheses are then tested to see which are valid and which are not. Other scientists double check this by trying to replicate the original researcher's work. It is by this process that we slowly accumulate knowledge about the way the world really works. There is a definite right and wrong and we know for certain how many phenomena really and truly work.

Scholars of scientific method believed this idealized classroom version for many years, and who can blame them given the evidence of tremendous technological advance? But closer examination reveals several problems. Start first with the subject matter. Is the world really out there in some objective form, waiting for us to discover its secrets? Or are we actually putting our own particular interpretations on what we see? The quick answer is that it is no doubt a bit of both – but especially the latter. To understand this, consider for a moment the philosophical query, "If a tree falls in the forest and no one is around to hear it, does it make a sound?" One is usually told that there are a number of potential answers and that these depend on your perspective and assumptions. Teasing out the latter is the point of the exercise. But, strictly speaking and assuming "no one" also excludes animals from being within earshot, there is only one correct response: no. This is because "sound" does not exist in the absence of ears (or similar organs). Our ears translate the vibrations in the air into impulses that we interpret as sound. If there are no ears, there is no sound.

Thus, while it might be safe to say that one of the consequences of a tree falling in the forest is the creation of vibration in the air, it is not sound unless there are ears in the vicinity. Sound is just our human-centered (or ear-centered) interpretation of it. Our version of what happened is, quite naturally, biased by what we are equipped to notice. For all we know, there may be a whole range of fascinating and important phenomena associated with tree falling of which we are totally ignorant, things that would be noticed by dogs, eagles, bats, ants, microscopes, thermometers, seismographs, extra terrestrials, and so on. We do not, therefore, collect "facts," only our limited impressions of the phenomena we are capable of noticing.

It is not just our senses (or those scientific tools used to enhance them) that affect our perspective. We are social animals. We hunt, mate, feed, and so on in packs. We also instinctively want to share the culture (values, mores, world views, practices) of our pack, as this is what binds us together and makes us feel safe. Returning to how science is done, since cultures differ, this creates even more room for varying interpretations of the phenomena we experience. The world around us is filtered first by our physical capabilities and then by our cultural proclivities.

To offer a simple example, take the fable of "The Boy Who Cried Wolf," attributed to the Greek storyteller Aesop. A young shepherd is guarding his flock in an isolated pasture and is very lonely and bored. He decides to call out, "Wolf!" so that the townspeople will rush out to help him. They do so, which relieves his boredom, but when they arrive he tells them that the wolf is already gone. They go back to town, until he repeats this very same cry for help the next day and the next. Each time, they hurry to the pasture, only to be told that the wolf has just left. On the fourth day, a wolf really does attack the flock and the shepherd calls out once again; but the increasingly suspicious townspeople do not come. They assume it is another of his lies, and the boy and his flock are devoured.

In cultures where this story is told, the intended lesson is that if you continually lie, no one will believe you even if you are telling the truth. The moral is that we should always be honest. However, on the science fiction television program, *Star Trek: Deep Space Nine*, this same story is told to a member of an alien species called the Cardassians. Their fictitious culture is a very Spartan one in which victory at any price is highly praised. Friendships and honesty are not valued as much as success and cunning. Hence, when the human, Dr Bashir, self-righteously announces the moral of the story to the Cardassian, Elim Garak, the latter replies with, "Are you sure that's the point, Doctor?" Dr Bashir responds, "Of course, what else could it be?" to which Garak suggests, "That you should never tell the same lie twice."

Garak's implication that the fable could just as easily be used to illustrate Cardassian values is quite right. But if that is true, then the moral itself must not be inherent to the story. Rather, each observer "learned" from the tale only what he already believed in the first place. For Dr Bashir, the fact that the liar in the story is punished is consistent with his culture's view; for Garek, it shows, as Cardassians believe, that one must be cunning – had the boy only concocted more imaginative lies, he might have both survived and relieved his loneliness. Yet a third observer could have argued that the story illustrated the folly of entrusting dangerous jobs to children or that a cry for help should never be ignored. What you see is strongly influenced by what you expect to see. As the economist Gunnar Myrdal was fond of saying, "There can be no view except from a viewpoint" (Myrdal 1978, p. 779).

These issues of bias are not limited to stories about falling trees and shepherds. Those who study research in the natural sciences, where one would imagine that these problems would have the least impact, have nevertheless found that scientists tend to design studies in a manner that makes them more likely to "discover" precisely what they expected to find in the first place. This need not be intentional and in some ways it is unavoidable. If you suspect that a chemical process may generate heat, then you set up a thermometer to measure it; but if you do not expect it, then you may not use a thermometer at all and an important side effect might go unnoticed. You design your experiment to record what you expect to see, which makes it more likely that you will see it (and not something else). In the words of Albert Einstein, "Whether you can observe a thing or not depends on the theory which you use" (Salam 1990, p. 99).

None of this precludes scientific progress, of course. It must not, or we would not have powered flight, penicillin, plumbing, or the printing press. It just shows that the process is not as straightforward as you were taught when you were younger. The fact is that scientists are people too, with the same strengths and weaknesses as the rest of us.

A REALISTIC VERSION OF SCIENCE

If scientists are not uncovering objective facts, then what are they doing? The first step in answering that question is the realization that real-life science is in itself a subculture that consists of a bundle of world views, values, practices, and behavioral standards.[1] It exists inside a larger culture, with which there will be varying degrees of overlap and conflict. In that sense, what we call "science" is no different from Buddhism, dentistry, Rastafarianism, online computer gaming, antique collecting, or any other group that shares behavioral norms and common practices. It is not a-cultural or value-free, but a particular culture and a specific set of values. Roughly speaking, what really makes a scientist a scientist is the belief that the world can be understood via the systematic study of its observed characteristics and that skepticism, objectivity, and respect for logic and evidence are the values most likely to lead us to useful and reliable explanations. This is the essence of their subculture – not that they, like members of any other subculture, i ᷆ alwɒy successful in living up to their own ideals.

The communities of individuals who share those dealls extend across many different kinds of science and a number of distinct schools oɨ thought or paradigms ("school of thought" and "paradigm" will be used interchangeably in this book). Thinking specifically about economics (though most of this would apply generally), each school of thought consists of the following elements:

1. Formal Analytic Structure
   i. world view: ideological and philosophical lens through which members see the real world
   ii. axioms: unquestioned/unquestionable assumptions
   iii. methods: how the economy should be studied
   iv. provisional explanations: theories and models.
2. Recommended Applications of their research or policies.
3. Behavioral Standards each member is expected to follow in order to remain in good standing.

These are discussed at length below, with parenthetical references to the outline above to make following the discussion easier. In the process, a more realistic version of the science will be built.

The Formal Analytic Structure (section 1) consists of the world view, axioms, and methods shared by the community of scientists in question, plus the set of provisional explanations they have developed via their research (provisional because they are never final and always subject to review and revision or rejection). The world view (section 1.i) is a function of various cultural and ideological biases and it provides the lens through which the real world is seen and subsequent analyses are made. It includes the school of thought's views on the nature of humanity, its common social goal or sense of economic justice, and what members assume regarding the nature of economic inquiry (that is, their broad philosophical understanding of what it means to do research). Axioms (section 1.ii) are the unquestioned and, indeed, unquestionable concepts that every member of the school of thought accepts (for example, Neoclassicism's belief that economic agents are rational or Marxists' assumption that all history is a history of class struggle). Methods (section 1.iii) describe the acceptable or preferred means of studying phenomena in the paradigm (deduction, induction, surveys, interviews, statistical analysis, and so on).

Armed with the above, economists observe the world around them and determine which phenomena are of interest and therefore worthy of study. Religious, political, corporate, and other forces play a role in this process, as controversies surrounding stem-cell research and global warming have demonstrated. What is of interest is decided both socially and by the paradigm in question. Research is then the process of developing provisional explanations (section 1.iv) of these foci. These take the form of theories and models, where the former are conjectures regarding the nature of individual phenomena (for example, the theory of supply or the theory of demand) and the latter are sets of theories designed to explain some larger or more complex concept (for example, the market). Recall that what they are trying to explain does not consist of a set of immutable, innate characteristics within an objective universe. What economists perceive as the "real world" is a function of their world view and is thus a conceptualized, rather than objective, reality. It is impossible for it to be otherwise.

This bears repeating. Scientists cannot set out to discover objective facts since objective facts do not exist. We are inevitably limited to collecting and studying biased observations and interpretations of what we study. Under these circumstances, the best for which scientists can hope is to make some practical sense of what they see around them. But the good news is this more modest goal is not only within our grasp, it can be extremely useful. It means that we are able to develop working rules that enable us to interact successfully with our environment (broadly defined). Even though we can never, for a variety of reasons, declare any theory or model absolutely "correct," we can nevertheless make a case for a particular provisional explanation having been consistently useful or reliable. This is not insignificant. In fact, it is the actual pragmatic contribution of science to human welfare. We may never know if it is true that air traveling over a curved surface creates lift, but thus far that characterization has led us from the Wright brothers at Kitty Hawk to the National Aeronautics and Space Administration's (NASA) space shuttle. For all we know, our conceptualization of the process is deeply flawed and what is really occurring is related to forces that we do not even suspect exist. That has not, however, kept us from flying.

This is not to say that everything that may be useful and reliable will be accepted, however, and acceptance must occur if a theory or model is to enter the paradigm's formal set of provisional explanations. Utility and reliability are certainly important factors in that process, but they are by no means the only ones. There are many forces in society and science that affect a theory or model's popularity, some of which have no serious connection to its specific merits. It has already been suggested that the broader culture can shape scientific debate. History is full of examples, from evolution to stem-cell research and Galileo to Dr Kevorkian. Science and scientists are part of a larger social unit and are necessarily constrained by that connection. Not that science is slave to non-scientific influences; it is a two-way street, such that it both affects and is affected by the broader set of values. The ideals we generally associate with the scientific subculture may be inserted into the broader debate because those members of society who are scientists successfully argue that they should be. This is why Creationists find it necessary to supplement their religious positions with evidence regarding the fossil record. They feel obliged to at least appear to speak the scientists' language in order to be taken seriously.

Moving on to the next component of a school of thought, Recommended Applications or policies (section 2), these arise from the comparison of two segments from the first component. The social goals contained in the world view part of the Formal Analytic Structure (section 1.i) suggest what members of this paradigm think the world should look like, while the conceptualized reality from the provisional explanations (section 1.iv) shows how they think it really looks. If those are not the same, then some course of action will be suggested. Note that because these recommended applications or policies are informed by the school of thought's set of provisional explanations, two paradigms could perceive the exact same problem but recommend different solutions. For example, if unemployment is deemed to be unacceptably high, Post

Keynesians might argue that this calls for an employer of last resort policy. Neoclassicals, on the other hand, may suggest the repeal of minimum wage laws, while Marxists would argue that unemployment is a natural consequence of capitalism and will not end until the workers revolt. They could thus agree on the problem but disagree about the solution because their theories and models specify different lines of causation.

The final component is that associated with Behavioral Standards (section 3). While one will not find complete homogeneity within any subculture or individual school of thought, there are certain core values, practices, and beliefs that each member must follow to remain in good standing. These standards are violated at the risk of loss of status or expulsion. By contrast, conspicuous adherence may lead to increased prestige or promotion – and success in promoting particular models and theories, especially in terms of what is selected for publication. Primary and secondary standards are obviously related to the items under Formal Analytic Structure (section 1), but they are not identical. Roughly speaking, the latter represents what members of a school of thought say they value, the standards show what is really rewarded in practice. They may also highlight certain themes or emphases not otherwise evident from the Formal Analytic Structure (section 1). Secondary standards may be violated within certain limits, but primary ones are to be obeyed or you are not "one of us."

Take physicians as an example. For the sake of argument, assume that most members of this group are political conservatives who enjoy playing golf and reading mystery novels. Not sharing one or more of these interests might mean that a particular physician is less popular with her peers, but no one would deny that she is still a physician. Violation of these secondary standards make participating in the subculture more difficult (as you find yourself excluded from various professional activities, for example), though not impossible. If, however, she decides to start making diagnoses on the basis of star signs and planetary alignments, her behavior could lead to formal investigation and a loss of license. This is true even though among astrologists (or physicians of a different century), such behavior would be considered perfectly appropriate. However, a primary standard of modern medicine is that disease is related to human physiological conditions and not to the relative positions of heavenly bodies. She is perfectly free to disagree on the bases that take primary standards as given. For example, she could offer a contrary opinion based on her analysis of a patient's biochemistry, the interpretation of a lab result, or the examination of an x-ray. None of these, alone, would be viewed as un-physicianly. But if she persists in arguing that her patient is ill because "Venus is ascending," then she is out of the club. She is no longer a physician.

Returning to the secondary standards, even egregious violations need not lead to dismissal, though they may harm your reputation. Say, for example, our physician decides to start coming to work in cut-off jeans, a t-shirt, and sandals. This may be viewed as unprofessional by both colleagues and patients; by itself, however, this may have no significant consequences. Or she could recommend herbal remedies to patients. So long as this is alongside standard prescriptions, little may be said. Replacing the couches and armchairs in her waiting room with bean bag chairs might cause a murmur, but she is still a physician. However, violation of all three of these at once – wearing cut-off jeans, a t-shirt, and sandals, recommending herbal medicines, and decorating the waiting room with bean bag chairs – will raise some concern within the physician subculture. Depending on her status in the medical community and the existence of offsetting positives (perhaps she is universally recognized as a brilliant diagnostician, in which case her transgressions may be viewed as amusing eccentricities), she could well face sanctions and certainly a fall in status. She will probably not be elected as the next president of the American Medical Association.

This is significant for the subject of this book because adherence to standards has an impact on the chances that an economist's work is published. As will be discussed later, journal articles and books represent the primary means by which we communicate with each other, develop new theories and models, critique and amend existing ones, and so on. However, those unable to win the approval of the gatekeepers by adhering to the established standards may not join the conversation.

Standards really do not, incidentally, have to be forced on anyone. To begin with, those who consciously elect to join a subculture are probably predisposed to conform to those particular norms. If not, then the values in question can take hold as interaction with other members occurs. This is particularly likely when there is an initiation process, a sizeable investment to become accepted, or a significant reward for being associated with the subculture. Any doubts can be swept away by sincere conversion or the desire to believe. But even if one remains unconvinced, being a member at least requires paying lip service to the primary standards (and most secondary ones). A physician who truly believes that her patient is ill because he is a Virgo must, if she is to keep her license, keep this to herself and offer a diagnosis that is consistent with accepted medical practice. Standards can evolve, of course, but this generally takes a long time and unusual circumstances. Powerful personalities, strong external forces, and so on may be involved, and it is just as likely that these lead to a new subculture (or school of thought) than a change in the existing one. Institutions resist change.

Returning to a point raised above, Behavioral Standards (section 3) and the Formal Analytic Structure (section 1) of the paradigm are related but necessarily distinct concepts. The latter represents what those in a school of thought say they do, while the standards are closer to what they actually do. In certain branches of Neoclassical economics, for example, their methodology places a great deal of weight on the predictive power of models. In practice, however, such tests are exceedingly rare. Not only is one not really expected to present this sort of evidence in defense of a theory (in a published article, for example), but the absence of such a tradition makes it difficult to even imagine how it would be done. For the student of economic paradigms, this is enlightening because it is an important guide to what, in practice, really makes a theory or model acceptable. This is hardly a situation confined to Neoclassicism. Every school of thought has things they say are important to them, but which in reality they do not pursue.

Second, the Behavioral Standards (section 3) are distinct from the Formal Analytic Structure (section 1) in the sense that they give insight regarding something that the latter does not: hierarchies within the school of thought. Not every concept is considered equally important. Focusing one's work in a legitimate but, in the minds of your colleagues, inconsequential area will make it very difficult to contribute provisional explanations that will win acceptance and raise your status in the community. This implicit ranking manifests itself particularly in the secondary standards, and it exerts a strong influence over what research is done and which models and theories become popular.

Third, because a school of thought's world view, axioms, methods, and models and theories are more likely to have been carefully and self-consciously developed, they will have a greater tendency to be internally consistent and instrumental in achieving their stated goals. But standards evolve more subtly and need not have any pragmatic aim. For example, you will not find any contractions in this book because they are considered unprofessional in scholarly writing. Does it actually make my argument more powerful to have said "will not" rather than "won't" in the previous sentence? Of course not – in fact, it would have saved a bit of printer's ink! This is a ceremonial standard that not only serves no instrumental purpose, but can actually obstruct it. Such rules are, nevertheless, taken very seriously and they guide group behavior every bit as much as those that are more pragmatic.

Again, this is not to say that the utility and reliability of an explanation are unimportant, only that consistency with social and paradigmatic standards (primary and secondary) is also critical and cannot be ignored when trying to understand how theory evolves. In addition, there may be structural factors that affect which standards are most vigorously enforced and which schools of thought and social groups are best placed to make their views *the* views of the discipline as a whole. The editorship of journals and management of graduate programs are key in this respect, while in society, in general, those who are most powerful will be in the best position to encourage the science that is consistent with their interests. Not too many Fortune 500 companies fund centers for Marxist economic research, though it would not be surprising to see them underwriting a professorship in free enterprise (the reverse of the priorities of elites in the Soviet Union). Those pursuing research agendas inconsistent with powerful social or scientific interests, regardless of how promising they may be in terms of utility and reliability, face an uphill battle. Any reasonable explanation of the evolution of theory, economic or otherwise, must be multidimensional and must consider more than just utility and reliability (Mackie 1998). It would be comforting to think that the best ideas always win, but the world is not that simple.

The conclusion is that real science is not some coldly rational institution, slowly stamping out ignorance and replacing it with the truth about the objective world around us. It cannot be, because no one is impartial and there is no objective world. Instead, real science is a necessarily imperfect attempt to generate practical explanations of our biased observations. It is the scientist's hope that others will accept these as reasonable. This is not meant to imply that science is a pointless exercise dominated by superstition and vested interests. Far from it, the subculture that values skepticism, objectivity, logic, and evidence has brought us many tangible benefits. But it has done so while operating under a number of constraints, some unavoidable, some external, and some internal. The state of economic theory today cannot be understood independent of these forces.

ECONOMICS: TRAINING AND APPRENTICESHIP

Economists are members of the larger subculture of scientists. They share with them the belief that the world can be understood via the systematic study of its observed characteristics and that skepticism, objectivity, and respect for logic and evidence are the values most likely to lead us to useful and reliable explanations. And they, too, are subject to the same sensory and cultural biases and external influences. What differ are the subject matter of their study and the nature of the internal forces, including primary and secondary standards, that affect their inquiry. With respect to the former, economics is anything associated with human social activities related to our wellbeing, especially as related to the production and distribution of goods and services and the allocation of resources. Such phenomena range from currency prices to antitrust legislation and from professional athletes' salaries to gender roles in the household. Contrary to popular belief, economics is not just about markets. Historical and contemporary economies dominated by command or tradition are of great interest too. Nor is it only about scarcity of resources. The Great Depression, for example, was marked by an excess of the most important resource in the economy: labor. While some individual schools of thought may employ a more limited definition, "economics" actually encompasses a wide variety of activities.

Explaining the internal forces and primary and secondary standards governing our discipline requires a relatively detailed outline of the structure of the profession, including the manner in which economists are trained, the nature of their work, and how an individual enters the larger intellectual discussions that determine the course of theory. This will take some time, but I hope readers will find that this practical explanation, emphasizing the day-to-day activities of the professional economist, gives them a much better feel for how our discipline really works and where schools of thought exist. All this has an important impact on what sort of provisional explanations are developed and which ones become accepted, which is of course a major subject of this book.

Before proceeding, note first that while the following is meant to apply to economics in general, by necessity it leans toward the practices followed by the school of thought that is most influential in setting standards in the profession: Neoclassicism. This is not altogether in-appropriate as almost every single economist in the world, regardless of the route she eventually chose, was initially trained as a Neoclassical. This is also primarily a description of the system as it exists in the United States. However, those aspects emphasized here should be similar enough in other countries that this should not create an insurmountable problem. Note, too, that no attempt is made to identify the components of a common formal analytic structure (world view, axioms, methods, theories, and models) that all economists believe. Though I am sure this could be accomplished, it would have to be very general and the fact that the rest of the book then focuses on how schools of thought differ on those very topics may make such an effort more confusing than illuminating. There are many common standards, however, and these will be outlined here and their effect on the discipline discussed. Last, remember that there is no such thing as a view except from a view point. Hence, while

I have tried very hard to remain objective in my analysis, that is not the same as saying that I am neutral. In point of fact, I think that the current system is broken. This is so because it does not generate the vigorous debate among schools of thought that the imperfect nature of scientific inquiry requires for the development of useful and reliable explanations. Since it is not true that scientists are unbiased protectors of truth, provisional explanations should be regularly and openly challenged – especially by those from opposing paradigms. This is extremely rare in real life. The primary and secondary behavioral standards and specific structure of modern economics instead create incentives that encourage conformity and monism (that is, the belief that only one legitimate view exists). Institutional inertia takes over and muffles criticism and, in extreme cases, punishes those with contrary opinions with banishment – they are no longer considered economists. Very little real significant debate takes place in our discipline. The review that follows reflects this criticism.[2]

The beginning of economics is traditionally dated to 1776, the year that Adam Smith's *An Inquiry into the Nature and Causes of the Wealth of Nations* was published. However, it was not until the late 1800s that it emerged as an academic discipline unto itself (Mackie 1998, p. 7). Today, the training and apprenticeship of the economist has become highly formalized.[3] This begins at the undergraduate level, where education is dominated by the textbook approach (Clower 1989, pp. 27–8). The advantage is the standardization of course material across universities and the fact that it suggests that an effort has been made to make the concepts accessible to students. In addition, the existence of a text means that a new preparation is easier to develop, which is particularly good news to the brand-new faculty member. The disadvantage is the tendency to avoid anything that might harm sales: controversial, unique, and complex subjects, for example. New ideas, too, may take a long time to reach texts. In addition, it may stifle innovation as instructors accustomed to this culture may avoid creating courses for which a ready-made textbook does not already exist. These factors combine to create a tendency for undergraduate education to be somewhat generic and potentially bland because the textbook culture encourages aiming at the lowest common denominator. This is most likely to be a problem at the introductory level where the market is largest. There are energetic and enthusiastic instructors who will find means to enhance the classroom experience and there are good textbooks, but they face these constraints.

In terms of subject matter, the central focus is on teaching students "how to think like an economist." What this means is learning to evaluate alternatives in a formalized cost-benefit framework and to consider the incentives facing individuals and how these might create unanticipated consequences. This is often described in terms of immutable and universally accepted laws and concepts like self-interest, utility maximization, demand, supply, comparative advantage, equilibrium, rationality, and so on. These will be organized into formal models and applied to a variety of situations, with advanced classes (international economics, labor, economic history, and so on) presenting specific applications of the common tools to new topic areas. In most programs it is emphasized that economics is, in contrast to what was said earlier in this chapter, value-free. The discipline is thus described to students as one in which all analyses are completely objective, the core concepts are acknowledged as facts, and controversies concern only matters of degree. In such a world, there is no point in discussing alternative schools of thought because they must have already been harvested for their useful ideas. As in the simplistic version of science discussed earlier in the chapter, the current state of economic theory is presented as the result of a steady and progressive process of separating fact from fiction wherein a single school of thought totally and appropriately dominates the conversation. Note that the textbook culture fits nicely with this since it prefers standardization.

This does not describe every program, but it is the common base from which any variations arise. Those who approve of this state of affairs argue that students learn to use a sophisticated set of tools to analyse novel situations in a discipline that has consistently and successfully worked to replace bad theory with good. Indeed, it is true that economics majors are always among the high scorers on graduate placement exams (particularly in logic and mathematics) and there is evidence that they are also among those who advance the most quickly in the workplace. If something is broken in the economics major, proponents say, then it is difficult to see what is based on these results. It is a rigorous discipline that is feared by many students. Those who select economics take a certain pride in this.

Not everyone is so enthusiastic, however, and they worry in particular that portraying our discipline as completely objective and free of controversy is not only false, but it leaves students at "the stage of dualism, where all questions are viewed in black and white with decidedly right and wrong answers" as opposed to moving them to "higher stages of cognitive development (multiplicity, contextual relativism, and contextually appropriate decisions)" (McGoldrick 2009, p. 222; see also Becker 2007; Butler 2009). Reliance on multiple-choice exams may also contribute to this naivete (Becker and Johnston 1999). This view implies that while the average economics major graduates with excellent problem-solving skills, whether or not she is equipped to understand where to apply them, what limitations they may have, and when other approaches might be more appropriate is an open question.

Regardless of the strengths and weaknesses of this approach, some students (including your author) emerge from the undergraduate experience with a desire to become an economist. To do so, particularly one who is able to contribute provisional explanations to the body of existing knowledge, one must almost certainly earn a PhD. In the United States, this requires taking the Graduate Record Exam and sending off transcripts and applications to various universities. Depending on career aspirations and desired areas of emphasis, the hopeful may also consult one of the many departmental rankings that exist. Once accepted, the PhD candidate will find that many of the classes sound very similar to those offered in her undergraduate curriculum. These may include macroeconomic and microeconomic theory, labor economics, public finance, international trade and payments, and so on. There are also courses not necessarily offered to those earning bachelor's degrees: econometrics, mathematical economics, game theory, and so on. And some classes, particularly those associated with the history of economics and economic history, are conspicuous by their absence. This is a function of the heavy shift toward developing advanced mathematical skills. This is evident not only from the mix of courses but also in the content of those that, on the surface, remained the same. An undergraduate international trade class, for example, might consist of a mixture of graphically and algebraically presented theory and institutional detail. At the graduate level, the latter may be almost entirely absent, while the theories are now explained using matrices and calculus. This transformation is so complete that 57 percent of graduate students surveyed counted "excellence in mathematics" as very important to success in their program, while only 3 percent gave "having a thorough knowledge of the economy" the same rating (Klamer and Colander 1990, p. 18). One student commented: "You can walk in off the street and take the courses and not know what the Fortune 500 is and blaze through with flying colors. You can also come in and know the difference between subordinated debentures and junk bonds and fail miserably" (Klamer and Colander 1990, p. 18).

Though some economists view this as problematic, many others do not. In the typical graduate program, students learn the implicit lesson that what people say and what they do are not necessarily the same. Hence, relying on surveys, testimony, personal recollections, or any other form of qualitative data is seen as inherently suspect. This skepticism is extended to institutional and historical detail. Their inherent bias may serve, it is argued, to cloud rather than illuminate the issue. Hence, economists should rely on abstract reasoning and intuition. But, so as to ensure that this does not become uncontrolled speculation, it is expressed in advanced mathematics. This, they believe, provides the rigor necessary to apply basic economic principles to complex problems while at the same time maintaining objectivity. It is also the unstated reason for the move away from history and institutions and toward regressions and equations. Some schools of thought disagree strongly with this methodological position, saying that bad ideas expressed in advanced mathematics are still bad ideas – the math alone cannot change that fact; but it is nevertheless part of the economist's standard training in most programs. A self-selection process takes place whereby those who find this shift too challenging, uninteresting, or unconvincing leave. Those who remain have either fully endorsed the methodological principles implicit in this approach or are willing to endure until they have earned their degree.

In the United States, course work fills about the first two years of the PhD candidate's curriculum. Note that this level of education is much less textbook-oriented, with many journal articles – the primary means of communication among academic economists – assigned as class reading. Homework and projects are relatively rare, as exams and papers are the preferred method of evaluation. During this time, the student may also be serving as a teaching or research assistant or, somewhat later, an independent classroom instructor. And they will likely be attending seminars where drafts of professional papers are presented by in-house or visiting professors. It is by this process that the student is being introduced to the values and practices of the subculture of the professional economist. Through formal and informal channels, personal interactions with peers and professors, observations, class work, and so on, they are beginning to learn and internalize the primary and secondary standards of the economics profession.

One of the most basic secondary standards is that research is respected over teaching. This does not mean that individual faculty do not necessarily admire the creative and hard-working instructor, but there is definitely a hierarchy. Someone who is a successful researcher while lacking classroom skills is almost certain to earn a higher salary and garner more professional respect than the outstanding teacher who never publishes. Part of the rationalization is that research has the potential to reach many more people and lives than teaching, although in reality the overwhelming majority of it does not. In a world where 34,573 journal articles were published in 2008 alone (as reported by EconLit), one has to wonder how many of those had any impact whatsoever. A more pragmatic reason to value research is that economists who publish regularly are more likely to keep up with developments in their field. Once you earn your PhD, you are on your own. There are no refresher courses or periodic exams you must take. However, if you are able to publish your research, then this may indicate a continued mastery of your specialization. Well-published faculty might also be more likely to move beyond the textbook approach and build a course that would be relevant and interesting for the student. Even at institutions where research is not the top priority, this is obviously a plus. Of course, requiring faculty to research is not the only means of achieving this end, but it is the easiest for the university to employ (particularly as they do not have to manage the process by which research is evaluated and published).

Some worry, though, that the focus on research may have become more ceremonial than instrumental. Whether or not this is true is difficult to say, but it is certainly easy to imagine such a situation arising for a number of reasons. First, research is competitive – just because you enter the game, does not mean that you will succeed. In fact, most do not. A publication is, therefore, a trophy in a way that a classroom preparation is not. In that way, they would naturally serve to create distinctions among faculty members. In addition, such trophies are easy for administrators to count in determining promotions and raises, particularly in contrast to trying to evaluate faculty teaching (a bit more on this later). Note also that if research forms the primary means of promotion, then those making policy will generally be among the best-published members of the university community. They would have a strong desire to want to believe that research is important. Last, inasmuch as humans tend to emulate the behavior of the most respected members of our subculture, this creates a tendency for even teaching-oriented schools to want to become a miniature Massachusetts Institute of Technology (MIT) or Harvard. This means publishing, regardless of whether this serves an instrumental end.[4]

As implied above, that hierarchy applies to institutions as well as individuals. Rankings of academic departments are based not on teaching skill but number of publications and citations. In addition, there are preferred topic areas. High-level or more general theory is thought to be more impressive than policy-oriented or applied work, the use of advanced mathematics is considered superior to institutional or historical detail, and research in certain schools of thought and topic areas is regarded as better than that in others.

Students will absorb all this in classes and other interactions and this newfound knowledge about the standards of the discipline will be put to use in starting the dissertation. This begins after the course work and comprehensive exams in the chosen fields are complete (by about the start of the third year). First, with the help of one or more faculty members, the student writes a proposal. This is then formally presented and defended before a committee of professors selected by the student. They will evaluate its significance and feasibility relative to the candidate's need to prove her ability to conduct independent research according to current disciplinary standards. Once the proposal has been successfully defended (possibly with numerous amendments offered by the faculty), the student sets to work.

The dissertation usually requires two to five years, during which the student may take a course or two but will focus largely on writing. She will probably also be teaching her own classes. The dissertation itself may consist of a single, book-length thesis or a number of shorter ones (the former being the more traditional route, the latter better reflecting current professional norms). With the continuous advice and critique of her committee, the student develops her argument while being careful to follow the standards of the discipline. This is especially important if she plans a career in academics, where she will almost certainly be required to publish (as suggested above). If she can get an article or two out of her dissertation, it will be a big help to her early in her career.

Many students never finish their dissertation.[5] It takes a great deal of self-discipline to write something for which there is no deadline and no teacher pressuring you. Your committee members have their own work to do, and while the vast majority are very happy to help their charges by reading and commenting on various drafts, this represents a lot of extra (largely unrewarded) work for them. So, the responsibility lies solely with the student. But as the goal is to test the ability to conduct independent research, this seems not altogether inappropriate.

If a student does finish, the last formal step is the dissertation defense. Assuming that all members have already read and approved of the work, this may be largely a formality (even then, difficult questions might be posed as part of a ritualistic rite of passage). If successful, there are handshakes, hugs, and pats on the back as a new member is admitted to the "tribe." If not, the student goes off to revise.

Those who emerge with PhD in hand are now formally economists. The next step is finding employment. Many will seek jobs in academia, though there are numerous opportunities in the private sector and government. As the latter generally do not contribute to the development of theory, they will not be discussed here. It is at universities where most research is conducted, with some important work done in think tanks as well.

Entering academia usually means becoming a professor. At educational institutions in the United States, new PhDs are typically hired at the assistant professor level. Their responsibilities will fall into three primary areas: teaching, research, and service. The weights placed upon these vary considerably by university but, roughly speaking, the more classes you are expected to teach (usually two to four a semester), the more relaxed the research expectation. However, as suggested above, since the latter can be counted in a way that is not possible with the former, it usually plays the most visible role in any setting. Note that even though the pressure of graduate school is gone, this is still a tense period for many economists as they are technically on probation until around their sixth year. At that point, they are expected to present a portfolio of teaching, service, and research accomplishments that will convince the university to grant them promotion to associate professor (one short of the highest rank of full professor) and tenure. The privileges associated with tenure vary somewhat, but it basically means that it becomes much more difficult to be fired. Ideally, this is supposed to protect academic freedom in the sense that one cannot be terminated for teaching or researching unpopular or controversial topics.[6] This is obviously a major decision for both parties. For the candidate, if she is unsuccessful, then she must leave the university and look for new employment. For the university, they want to do their best not to tenure someone who will later prove to be unproductive. The probationary period can be a very important part of an economist's life. It is the apprenticeship phase that sets into motion patterns that continue throughout her career.

Without question, the most challenging part of the portfolio-building process is research. Service work is not only easy to find if one so desires, but it is rated relatively low anyway. No one who performs competently in teaching and research is going to be denied tenure on the basis of not having served on enough committees. Teaching is a great deal more demanding and preparing several new classes can be very time-consuming. This is particularly true because graduate programs rarely spend much, if any, effort on teaching their students how to teach. It is not a priority since earning a PhD in economics does not necessarily mean a career in academics. As a consequence, the brand-new professor will have to expend considerable effort crafting her courses and discovering and developing her personal skill set. For some, this is a pleasant and successful journey; for others, it is not.

How this is reflected in the portfolio is difficult to say. I do not want to suggest that universities do not take the teaching requirement seriously – many, if not most, certainly do. But, as suggested at several points above, it is very difficult to quantify the classroom skills of an instructor, especially with sufficient confidence to justify terminating someone's employment. Are poor student evaluations an indicator of insufficient time spent in class preparation or a fair but demanding instructor? Even if we have our suspicions, this is a very serious decision. With the best will in the world, it is simply very difficult for university officials to measure the quality of teaching. To some extent, they rely on self-selection – newly minted PhDs who do not enjoy time spent in front of students will probably not apply for jobs at colleges that require heavy teaching loads. Other forms of pressure can and will be applied too. But, in the end, it is relatively difficult to deny tenure on the basis of poor teaching alone.

Research, however, is a different story. It can easily be counted, sorted, and ranked. Even better, the evaluative bodies responsible for approving or rejecting submissions are external and composed of recognized authorities in the faculty member's discipline. Whether or not a faculty member gets a paper accepted by a journal has nothing to do with the university. The editor, probably a well-known and widely published economist, will receive the submission and make a preliminary evaluation. If the topic area does not fit what the journal publishes or if it is obviously unprofessional, the editor will reject it outright. Otherwise, the author's name will be removed and the submission sent to several economists who are experts in the relevant area. At this point, anywhere from a month to a year (or more) may pass while the referees review the paper.[7] When they are finished, each will send the editor a critique along with a recommendation. The standard range includes reject, revise and resubmit, accept with minor revisions, and accept without revision. The majority of papers (on the order of 75–90 percent) will receive one of the first two. The editor will consider her referees' evaluations and decide how to proceed. She has the last word.

Authors of accepted papers will rejoice, for they now have something to add to their portfolios. The sole fact of having written and submitted a paper would have counted for next to nothing. Likewise, presentations of original research at professional conferences, institutes, or other universities are nice as fillers in the candidate's application, but no number of these would be viewed as substituting for a publication. Nor would writing for a general, non-scientific audience be helpful. In addition, in economics (though not necessarily in other fields), book chapters or even entire books are not treated as the equivalent of a journal article because only the latter goes through the rigorous process of peer review by an editor and a team of experts (the place where the standards of behavior are most vigorously enforced). One must have their seal of approval to build a portfolio that will guarantee tenure and promotion. Many departments also employ strict rankings such that only publications in a handful of select journals give any real credit toward tenure. The recipient of a revise and resubmit will almost certainly do so, hoping that the second round will end in her favor. Those whose papers were rejected must decide if the manuscript is salvageable and, if so, whether to rewrite it before sending it to a different journal and playing the waiting game all over again. Depending on how close the individual is to the tenure decision, this can be a very tense and frustrating period.

Near the end of the probationary period, candidates submit their completed portfolios. These generally cycle up from the department to the college to the university, with various administrators and faculty evaluating the materials along the way. Successful candidates are promoted to associate professor and given tenure. If they wish, they may remain at this rank for the rest of their careers. Otherwise, with the passage of an appropriate number of years (usually about the same number as the probationary period), the associate may apply for promotion to the final rank of full professor. The procedure is similar, but there is much greater emphasis on research and, of course, the unsuccessful candidate is not out of work. Indeed, she is free to try again once she has added to her portfolio.

The post-tenure career of the academic economist will continue to involve varying degrees of research, teaching, and service, but with less direct pressure to reach a particular threshold with respect to the first. One of the goals of the tenure process was to select only those who would willingly engage in the level of research appropriate to the given institution. Personal goals vary as some professors move into administration, others into more popular writing, and still others into even more scholarship. Theoretically, the tenured professor is free to pursue different paths, though the rank of full professor and various other important perks and privileges are still reserved for those most heavily involved in research.

ECONOMICS: SCHOOLS OF THOUGHT

These, then, are the people primarily responsible for the development of economic theory. After their formal training, which takes place over roughly ten years of undergraduate and graduate education, they may participate in the academic discourse that occurs in our discipline. This discourse is usually segregated by school of thought and takes place in essentially two places: scholarly literature and the conferences organized by professional associations. The former is generated by journals and book publishers, each of which tends to specialize in a particular economic paradigm or subject area. The *Journal of Economic Issues*, for example, is an Institutionalist journal, *Science and Society* publishes Marxist work, and the *American Economic Review* focuses on Neo-classical theory. Each school of thought may also recognize an unofficial hierarchy of the journals in which they publish. Economists wanting to stay abreast of developments would look first to the leading journals in their school of thought. These are the face and front line of every paradigm and it is also where you want your work to be seen. Though they tend to earn relatively less respect than articles, books can be important too. This is particularly likely if the author has already established a reputation in journals, or if it is a "classic" (one of the foundational volumes in that paradigm, for example).

The role of conferences and professional associations in the development of economic theory is less direct. The former are organized meetings of economists at which unpublished research is presented, usually in the form of a 15–20-minute oral report. Such gatherings vary from meetings of thousands at large hotels and convention centers to a few dozen in university classrooms. Participation requires the submission of a proposal to the conference organizer, often an officer in the relevant association. Presenters are organized into panels by topic and papers may be discussed by a conference volunteer or the audience members. It can be very formal or relaxed, spirited or sedate. Conferences and the associations sponsoring them are tied to specific schools of thought and subject areas just as much as journals and publishing houses are. Unlike the latter, however, their impact on theory is minimal. Conferences are largely social and the papers presented there, even if exciting and thought-provoking, are reaching a very small audience. The author hoping to gain more exposure for her ideas would likely send her presentation paper to a journal. Conferences do play an important role though. Even in the internet age, face-to-face interaction can be a uniquely effective means of facilitating the exchange of ideas, association planning (including that involving any related journals), and the establishment of professional contacts. But each school of thought really exists and evolves on the pages of books and (especially) journals. It is there that the meaningful conversations take place, even if we get PowerPoint previews in convention hotels.

Not that every published article has a significant impact. How can they, given the numbers cited earlier (over 34,000 journal articles in 2008)? Nor is this out of line with what most of the authors expect. The majority of what professional economists do is akin to what Thomas Kuhn called normal science: the relatively routine work of slowly accumulating detail in accord with the paradigm's established theory (Kuhn 1962). It may involve the application of core concepts to an unexplored area (Marxist ideas of class as related to gender issues) or the resolution of an open but not necessarily critical question (does Keynes's *General Theory* assume endogenous or exogenous money?). This sort of work can lead to lively and useful conversations, perhaps later resulting in significant insights; generally speaking, however, there are a great many articles that are relatively trivial in terms of their contribution to broad theory. These may still serve a purpose in terms of helping the author develop her professional skill set or as useful, if non-essential, components of a larger body of literature on some topic; but they do not end up on anyone's required reading list.

How does an article achieve the latter distinction? There is no single explanation other than to say that it proved "significant." But since significance is in the eye of the beholder (most importantly, a journal referee), this is hardly an unambiguous answer. What we can say is that a multiplicity of variables contribute (including some decidedly non-scientific ones) and that these are a function of the very same factors that determine whether research is published in the first place: primary and secondary standards. Applications of these deemed by the scientific community as particularly clever, timely, or unique take center stage, possibly as lead articles in the highest-ranking journals. They then inspire other authors, receive frequent citation, are assigned in class, and potentially change how economists think about some aspect of their work. This is how theory evolves. It is also how the standards may evolve. It has been mentioned on a number of occasions that while the acceptance of the primary ones is vital to the success of a provisional explanation, one may reject one or more of the secondaries and still achieve notoriety. The key is to justify that rejection in the context of the other standards. In fact, such an achievement might well serve to make the idea "significant" and it may eventually lead to a paradigm-wide revision of the list of standards. Or, it could cause a splintering of the school of thought into subgroups or an entirely new paradigm. History has been witness to both and it is impossible to predict a priori which will occur. Within Marxism, for example, Baran and Sweezy's (1966) classic study rejected one of Marx's core arguments regarding the trend of the rate of profit in capitalist economies. However, it did so in a way that complemented many of the other standards and it was, at least in some economists' opinions, more consistent with historical data.

There are limits to this, of course, as there must be something ultimately "Marxist" about Marxism (delineating this is the role of primary standards). But it gives a basic idea of how evolution in economics takes place. It is a result of a complex interplay among the paradigmatic and disciplinary standards, external forces, personalities, and the structure of the profession. A comment made earlier still stands, however: institutions resist change. Normal science is the dominant activity of our profession and most of our time is spent solving puzzles rather than rewriting economic theory.[8]

The example of Baran and Sweezy raises one more issue that should be addressed before detailing the standards that exist in the economics profession: the interplay between theory and evidence in the evolution of paradigms. It was noted above that their revision was viewed by some as actually more consistent with historical trends than Marx's original.[9] One may wonder if this sort of adjustment theory to fit real-world observations is common, and generally it is not. This is so first of all because, as noted repeatedly, institutions resist change. Approaching economics from a particular perspective can quite naturally lead, for instance, to one only noticing data that tend to confirm your view. And even if contrary evidence is detected, it takes a considerable accumulation to lead you to reject the school of thought in which you were trained, earned tenure, and established a reputation. Furthermore, what weight of evidence should we consider sufficient to force the alteration of a theory? Is one observation among thousands enough to indict a paradigm's core concepts or models? After all, ours is a discipline in which controlled experimentation is impossible and our data are always contaminated by the fact that everything else is never equal. There is no easy answer to this and it is because of this that one may see one school of thought arguing vehemently that another's explanations are completely inconsistent with real-world observations, while the latter sees no problem at all (and may, in fact, be accusing the first of the same crime). Ultimately, a school of thought's world view, axioms, methods, theories, models, and policy prescriptions must be consistent with the world they purport to explain if they are to be useful and reliable aids in solving economic problems. Determining the degree of consistency necessary, however, is very difficult, particularly given the realistic view of science wherein absolute objectivity is impossible and theory determines what we see. If this were not true, there would only be one school of thought (and this book would not be necessary!).

ECONOMICS: PRIMARY AND SECONDARY STANDARDS OF BEHAVIOR

Throughout this chapter the important role played by behavioral standards in determining the success and status of the economist has been emphasized. While they were already introduced in the earlier discussion of the education and career of the professor, they will be reviewed and more clearly specified here. Standards vary by school of thought, of course, but many are common to all economists.[10] The key primary ones are the subject matter (that is, you are not an economist unless you are doing "economics"), the belief that the world can be understood via the systematic study of its observed characteristics, and that skepticism, objectivity, and respect for logic and reason are the values most likely to lead to useful and reliable explanations. Someone convicted of not following these would suffer consequences. For example, those at the training stage would find that their instructors would not assign passing grades if they insisted on submitting as assignments short stories, analyses of plant biology, or apartment building designs – all worthy endeavors, but not economics. Likewise, the professor who drifted into these areas would find that, unless a very convincing link could be made, she is no longer considered an economist. The main gatekeepers in the latter case would be the journal editors, meaning that the cost of straying would be banishment from publication – a death sentence for the untenured professor. Quite right – why should an economics department tenure someone who has spent the last six years publishing in chemistry journals? She needs to find a new job.[11]

The pursuit of systematic study as guided by skepticism, objectivity, logic, and evidence is taken just as seriously, though it may be somewhat more difficult to prove violations than with issues of subject matter. Again, the enforcers will be the students' instructors at the undergraduate and graduate levels and journal editors thereafter. Failing to adhere to these standards is the equivalent of being "unscientific," a label that every self-respecting scientist obviously wants to avoid and something that would represent a real obstacle in gaining the approval of departments, associations, conferences, journals, and publishers.

While the specifics may vary from school of thought to school of thought, all share these primary standards in spirit. These are very basic and uncontroversial, and as such should serve as a common bond among economists of every sort. As an aside, recognizing these commonalities is extremely important if we are to transform our discipline into one marked by serious but respectful debate. Marxists and Austrians already know where they disagree, but they may need to be reminded of where they concur.

It is more difficult to identify a set of common secondary standards, but Table 2.1 attempts to do just that. Recall that these may be violated with little consequence if in small doses, particularly when there are offsetting factors. Strict adherence, on the other hand, can enhance one's position – students following them receive higher grades and professors earn more publications in prestigious outlets. As suggested above, the table uses the earlier description of the training and apprenticeship of the economist and summarizes the most important secondary standards introduced at each level. Those marked with a G apply generally across all schools of thought, while those with an N lean more (though not exclusively) toward Neoclassicism. The latter are included in what is otherwise intended to be a common description because Neoclassicism is the mainstream and dominant school of thought in economics. Thus, their standards are "the" standards of the discipline. In addition, almost every economist, regardless of eventual school of thought, was trained in a Neoclassical program. Your average Austrian, Feminist, and Post Keynesian was at one point taught that, as shown on Table 2.1, economics is "constrained optimization under scarcity." These ideas, even if rejected on a conscious level, may linger both because they were part of their original introduction to the discipline.[12] Furthermore, people have a psychological tendency to want to emulate those most successful in their subculture.

As Table 2.1 shows, much of the undergraduate experience is oriented toward defining the discipline: what is economics? Most generally, it is constrained optimization, where the central constraint is scarcity of resources. Within that context, economic behavior is described as lawlike and tending toward equilibrium. Systemic incentives will guide behavior and may lead to unanticipated consequences. Economists exhibit a strong preference for formalized modeling processes in portraying these behaviors, emphasizing logic and analytical skills in their application. Many students are taught that economics is objective and value-free and most emerge from the undergraduate program with the sense that theirs is the most rigorous and, therefore, most scientific of the social sciences. Exam responses, term papers, and other assignments that support these themes are likely to meet with approval from instructors. Those that do not are taking a risk.

Graduate school carries with it the same standards as undergraduate and then adds to them. Here, with the subject matter already clearly defined, the new lessons are related to method. Probably core are the emphasis on deduction over induction, the related lack of relative concern for the historical and institutional considerations in model assumptions, and the consequent need for mathematics to provide the rigor necessary for objective analysis. Students also become cognizant of the fact that general and abstract theories tend to be valued over specific or policy-oriented ones. They also learn their first lessons about the profession itself, the first of which is that research is king. It is the key determinant

Table 2.1   Secondary standards learned during training and apprenticeship

Undergraduate	Graduate	Apprenticeship (pre-tenure professor)
G: preference for formalized modeling processes	G: research as the most important indicator of the value of an economist or department	G: hierarchy of journals
G: economics as emphasizing the application of logic and analytical skills	G: preference for general theories over specific and theory over application	G: importance of journal articles over all other publication types
N: economics as the role of incentives and unanticipated consequences	G: ancestor worship in the form of citations that legitimize an argument by linking it to a respected name or publication	G: importance of high-brow research over low-brow research
N: economics as superior to other social sciences	N: deduction as preferable to induction due to inherent bias of the latter	
N: economics as objective and value-free	N: lack of concern for historical and institutional accuracy of model assumptions relative to other characteristics	
N: economic forces as tending toward equilibrium	N: advanced mathematics as a reliable method of avoiding unconstrained speculation and bias	
N: economic behavior as law-like or natural		
N: economics as constrained optimization under scarcity		

Note: G indicates a general standard across schools of thought. N indicates a largely (though not exclusively) Neoclassical standard usually included as part of the training process.

of status. Last, their first experience in independent research will introduce them to the power of ancestor worship! A very useful means of establishing one's credibility is citing certain authors, books, and journals (a phenomenon that is hardly limited to economics).

By the time the PhD has been earned, most relevant standards of behavior about the subject itself have already been learned and only professional ones remain. Top are the priority of journal research over all other forms of publication and the existence of a strict hierarchy of journals. Depending on the institution, there may be no more than a dozen or half dozen outlets that earn one significant progress toward tenure. Publishing for the general public is practically worthless and may even harm one's reputation. All these forces play an extremely powerful role in determining what gets published and taught. This means that they are also key in the evolution of theory.

I hope the reader does not get the impression that I am arguing against these standards. The truth is more complex. First, one cannot have an institution – rational or irrational, simple or complex, good or evil – without standards of behavior. They are what define the institution and create shared values and expectations. However, as suggested above, some standards are ceremonial and do not serve to advance the organization's ends, while others are instrumental in doing so. Hence, in studying an institution's standards, the goal is to determine which fall into the former category and which into the latter. In terms of economics, I would argue its primary standards are perfectly appropriate. I see no problem with setting as our goal the explanation of only a specific subset of observed behavior and I am a strong believer in the idea that the world can be understood via the systematic study of its observed characteristics and that skepticism, objectivity, and respect for logic and reason are the values most likely to lead to useful and reliable explanations. Furthermore, I find that though I have less universal agreement with the items marked G in Table 2.1, I do not, on the other hand, see these as unequivocally problematic. Can we, for example, really deny that some journals consistently publish more significant research than others or that general theories are generally more useful than specific ones? Nor, even though I am not a Neoclassical, can I say that I am not sympathetic to some of the items marked with an "N."

The deeper problem is, because of the structure of the training and apprenticeship process, how narrowly and strictly these standards are enforced. As suggested earlier, the imperfect nature of scientific inquiry should lead us to the conclusion that vigorous debate among a plurality of perspectives (assuming that each is faithful to the values of skepticism, objectivity, and respect for logic and evidence in the development of systematic studies) is the process most likely to generate useful and reliable explanations of economic phenomena. Instead, the incentives that exist in our discipline encourage monism when we need pluralism, consent when real progress is more likely with dissent.

This begins at the undergraduate level where the textbook culture, combined with Neoclassicism's tendency to portray economics as completely objective, teaches the student that there is one and only one school of thought. This continues through the graduate level by teaching a methodological approach most consistent with that one approach. But it really reaches its climax during apprenticeship, when the neophyte invests a tremendous amount of intellectual capital while trying to earn tenure. Building the most critical component of the assistant professor's portfolio, that related to research, is time-consuming, intellectually challenging, and uncertain. This is not the stage of one's career to be taking a lot of chances, particularly since it is also a time when one is so busy with new teaching and service responsibilities.[13] Strict adherence to primary and secondary standards is the rule for those who wish to survive. Later, one can take on the economics establishment and accepted theory – right now, you just need to get tenure! But after six years of following these rules and abiding by all primary and secondary standards, including, in particular, any journal rankings your department employs, the tenured economist is unlikely to stray. Doing so would not only entail cutting ties with any reputation already created, but it would mean the hard work of starting over again in a new area. If graduate school introduces the budding economist to our rules of the game, the process of earning tenure internalizes and cements them.

There is nothing wrong with this, of course, if those rules are well considered and effective in terms of achieving the university's, profession's, and society's goals. In fact, if science worked as in the naive view, these might represent an effective guard against the intrusion of subjective and extra-scientific influences. But that is not the case, and so behavioral standards that encourage conservatism and discourage innovation should, at the very least, give us pause for thought. In a world where bias, perception, politics, religion, and other subjective and non-rational forces inevitably impact theory development, is it pragmatic to discourage economists from exploring alternative perspectives by decreeing that the only worthwhile publications are those of the few journals that most vigorously defend one particular set of secondary standards?[14] Obviously, this book is premised on the answer to that question being a very strong "no." Just as you do not truly understand what is unique about your native language until you learn a second one, so no one trained in a single school of thought can reasonably claim to possess a deep and critical understanding of even her own paradigm's strengths and weaknesses. You must have at least some knowledge of the alternatives.

If Marxists, Feminists, Institutionalists, Post Keynesians, Austrians, and New Institutionalists are not crackpots, if these are instead intelligent, hard-working individuals who share with Neoclassicals a strong respect for systematic analysis, skepticism, objectivity, logic, and evidence, then they should – in fact, they need – to have a scholarly forum in which they converse. Unfortunately, the far more common situation is that members of one school of thought dismiss some or all of the others as unscientific and therefore unworthy of the time necessary to facilitate the exchange of ideas. For me, there is not a single paradigm from which I have not learned something unique and insightful. This does not mean that I think they are all correct any more than each of the competing diagnoses of a patient's disease can all be right. But, presumably, the method by which we cure our patient begins with an open discussion of the strengths and weaknesses of each theory, not the a priori suppression of all but one. The same is true of the economy.

CONCLUSIONS

Economists are scientists who study human social activities related to our material wellbeing. They believe that these can be understood via the systematic analysis of their observed characteristics and that skepticism, objectivity, and respect for logic and evidence are the values most likely to lead us to useful and reliable explanations. Economics, like science in general, is affected by sensory and cultural biases. In addition, because it is a social activity, the popularity of a theory or model involves more than just its ability to explain the phenomenon in question. It is also necessary to account for politics, personalities, prejudices, religion, vested interests, jealousies, and so on. To put it in Neoclassical microeconomic terms, these are the constraints under which we operate when trying to maximize our knowledge of the economy. This is inevitable, but those who consciously acknowledge the role of these factors are better placed to minimize their impact.

For every school of thought in economics, one can construct a formal paradigm. This is the object of the rest of the book. Primary and secondary standards of behavior will also be identified and their impacts explained. Some standards are shared across all paradigms because they arise from the common aspects of training, apprenticeship, and employment described above. Many others will be unique to that particular school of thought and will, by their nature, define the sort of research undertaken by those economists and which theories endure.

The reader should not expect that this volume will leave her feeling as if she is an expert in every school of thought or that she knows exactly where she stands in terms of her beliefs about how the economy works. Instead, it is far more likely that its effect will be to open many new questions. If her experience is typical, however, these will be burning questions that will ignite a strong desire to know more about our discipline and the world it purports to explain.

NOTES

1. While the term subculture usually implies the existence of certain counter-cultural elements, I am using the term more generally here. I merely mean some distinct subgroup within a larger culture.
2. I am not arguing that this is the fault of Neoclassicism, per se. The same situation could well have arisen in a world where Marxists or Austrians controlled the training of new economists and the major publication outlets, and it would be every bit as objectionable.
3. Recall how this tends to increase the degree to which the subculture's values are accepted by members, as will the rigor of the process and the benefits of membership.
4. This is not, incidentally, a personal complaint. My primary motivation for earning a PhD was to do research and I have been well served by our system. However, there is no reason to believe that what is good for John Harvey is good for economics!
5. According to the PhD Completion Project, just under one half of those in economics are still incomplete after the tenth year of graduate school (http://www.phdcompletion.org, accessed May 3, 2010). It would be safe to say that exceedingly few of those are ever finished. Of those who are done by year ten, 90 percent earned PhDs by year seven.
6. Though other forms of pressure could, and are, applied. At the University of Notre Dame, for example, those members of the economics faculty pursuing non-Neoclassical research were split off into a brand-new department (Economics and Policy Studies), which was shortly thereafter – and to no one's surprise – disbanded. This was despite the fact that those faculty were well published and had an excellent reputation among non-mainstream economists.
7. This is not to imply that a referee will work on a review for a year. Rather, different journals operate with different expectations and, generally speaking, the referee will procrastinate as long as the editor will allow!
8. For those familiar with Thomas Kuhn's work, note that while I am accepting his concept of normal science, I have not mentioned revolutionary science. This is because, like many others, I am skeptical regarding the existence of such paradigm shifts in our discipline. Perhaps these could be conceptualized as a change in the primary standards, but I would rather discuss them as such than attach the adjective "revolutionary" to them. The latter implies a much more significant event than we actually witness in economics. We tend to see the splintering of schools of thought, not massive changes from within.
9. In particular, Marx argued that profits would fall over time, while some argued that they appeared to be rising.
10. Note that there will continue to be a general bias toward Neoclassicism in what follows and that this will be amended as necessary in subsequent chapters.
11. More complex problems can arise, however, when one school of thought calls something "economics" that another does not. In this case, the professor can think she is following all the rules but discovers that particular journal editors or tenure committees disagree. This will become more clear in the chapters that follow.
12. In fact, research suggests that people subconsciously treat the first explanation they hear as the default one, even when they may reject it on a conscious level (Lakoff 2006a, 2006b).

13. It is also when one is really trying to tie together all the loose ends from graduate education. The undergraduate student may be surprised to learn how many brand-new PhDs are still struggling with their own understanding of the economy. A doctorate is not so much a certification that you are now an expert, but that you have learned the skills to figure out how to become one!
14. For an interesting debate over whether or not the current reward structure built into the publication process serves to efficiently evaluate theory, see Laband and Tollison (2000) and Yeager (1997, 2000). In summary, Laband and Tollison said that it did because the most financially successful journals must be offering a better product, while Yeager argued that popular and good were not the same thing.

REFERENCES

Baran, P.A. and P.M. Sweezy (1966), *Monopoly Capital: An Essay on the American Social and Economic Order*, New York: Monthly Review Press.

Becker, W.E. (2007), "Quit lying and address the controversies: there are no dogmata, laws, rules, or standards in the science of economics," *American Economist*, **51** (1), 3–14.

Becker, W.E. and C. Johnston (1999), "The relationship between multiple choice and essay response questions in assessing economics understanding," *The Economic Record*, **75** (231), 348–57.

Butler, A. (2009), "The illusion of objectivity: implications for teaching economics," in R.F. Garnett, E.K. Olsen, and Martha Starr (eds), *Economic Pluralism*, London: Routledge, pp. 236–49.

Clower, R.W. (1989), "The state of economics: hopeless but not serious?," in D.C. Colander and A.W. Coats (eds), *The Spread of Economic Ideas*, Cambridge: Cambridge University Press, pp. 23–9.

Klamer, A. and D. Colander (1990), *The Making of an Economist*, Boulder, CO: Westview Press.

Kuhn, T.S. (1962), *The Structure of Scientific Revolutions*, Chicago, IL: University of Chicago Press.

Laband, D.N. and R.D. Tollison (2000), "On secondhandism and scientific appraisal," *Quarterly Journal of Austrian Economics*, **3** (1), 43–8.

Lakoff, G. (2006a), *Whose Freedom? The Battle Over America's Most Important Idea*, New York: Farrar, Straus and Giroux.

Lakoff, G. (2006b), *Thinking Points: Communicating Our American Values and Vision*, New York: Farrar, Straus and Giroux.

Mackie, C.D. (1998), *Canonizing Economic Theory: How Theories and Ideas are Selected in Economics*, Armonk, NY: ME Sharpe.

McGoldrick, K. (2009), "Promoting a pluralist agenda in undergraduate economics education," in R.F. Garnett, E.K. Olsen, and M. Starr (eds), *Economic Pluralism*, London: Routledge, pp. 221–35.

Myrdal, G. (1978), "Institutional economics," *Journal of Economic Issues*, **12** (4), 771–83.

Salam, A. (1990), *Unification of Fundamental Forces: The First 1988 Dirac Memorial Lecture*, Cambridge: Cambridge University Press.

Smith, A. (1776), *An Inquiry into the Nature and Causes of the Wealth of Nations*, London: W. Strahan and T. Cadell, reprinted in 2004, Amazon Digital Services, Inc., Digireads.com.

Yeager, L.B. (1997), "Austrian economics, Neoclassicism, and the market test," *Journal of Economic Perspectives*, **11**, 153–65.

Yeager, L.B. (2000), "The tactics of secondhandism," *Quarterly Journal of Austrian Economics*, **3** (3), 51–61.

3. Neoclassical economics

Neoclassicism is the dominant school of thought in economics. Even those attending graduate programs known for their specialization in alternative paradigms will probably find that most of their classes are taught from this perspective. Part of the reason for this is the fact that, even at such institutions, it is often only a core group of faculty who are responsible for the department's non-Neoclassical reputation. The majority may still be in the mainstream and their courses are taught accordingly. But even barring that, many heterodox economists feel an obligation to cover orthodox topics, either in part or exclusively, so that their students will have sufficient background for the Neoclassical courses and programs that they may encounter elsewhere. Neoclassicism is also of central importance because of its role in policy. Almost every economic advisor and central banker in the world comes from this school of thought. Understanding the theory, practice, and teaching of modern economics absolutely requires understanding this school of thought. For all these reasons, it is covered first in this volume.

FOUNDATIONS OF NEOCLASSICISM: MARGINALISM AND SCOTTISH COMMON SENSE PHILOSOPHY

Modern Neoclassicism developed in the mid to late nineteenth century, roughly parallel to the emergence of economics as a professional academic discipline. The basic concepts, including marginal analysis, general equilibrium, rationality, price theory, and utility, were developed by a group of economists called the Marginalists: Alfred Marshall (1842–1924), William Stanley Jevons (1835–1882), Carl Menger (1840–1921), and Leon Walras (1834–1910). It is safe to say that almost everything in a modern microeconomics textbook can be traced back to or was inspired by these four scholars.

One of their motivations for developing an alternate theory was the desire to resolve a puzzle left over from the work of their precursors, the

Classical economists (for example, Adam Smith, David Ricardo, and Thomas Malthus). In an oft-quoted passage, Adam Smith (1723–1790) writes:

> The word value, it is to be observed, has two different meanings, and sometimes expresses the utility of some particular object, and sometimes the power of purchasing other goods which the possession of that object conveys. The one may be called "value in use;" the other, "value in exchange." The things which have the greatest value in use have frequently little or no value in exchange; and on the contrary, those which have the greatest value in exchange have frequently little or no value in use. Nothing is more useful than water: but it will purchase scarce any thing; scarce any thing can be had in exchange for it. A diamond, on the contrary, has scarce any value in use; but a very great quantity of other goods may frequently be had in exchange for it. (Smith 1776, p. 20)

This is the water-diamond paradox. Smith is asking, how can something so useful bring such a low price, while something so useless bring such a high one?

The answer to this question, according to the Marginalists, lies in analysing the problem from the point of view of the marginal, or last, unit of analysis. First, consider the utility (broadly understood as happiness) you gain from the consumption of some good or service. The Marginalists argued that this inevitably declines the more you consume within a given time period. The first piece of cake you eat after dinner, for example, is more satisfying than the second, the second more than the third, the third more than the fourth, and so on. In fact, if you continue to gorge yourself, you may soon discover that you are losing rather than gaining utility from additional units of cake. Had you been buying each piece of dessert then it is safe to say that you would have been willing to spend less for each subsequent slice. In other words, the value of the marginal (or last) unit is declining – and therein lies the key to the paradox.

Consider Figure 3.1. On the vertical axis it shows the additional utility (not the total) from consuming one more unit of the good in question and it assumes that this declines and can even become negative. The units of measure are irrelevant so long as it is made clear that water is, everything else being equal, more useful to us than diamonds. This is why the line for water is higher everywhere than that for diamonds, which is consistent with Smith's statement regarding value in use above. However, everything else is not equal, for the relative scarcity of the two products is such that our average consumer is able to enjoy Q2 units of water but only Q1 units of diamonds. This leaves the marginal utility of the former at MU2 and that of the latter at MU1. Hence, while water is generally more useful than diamonds, its value in exchange is far lower because what you are willing to pay is a function of how anxious you are to acquire the next unit – and you already have a great many units of water.

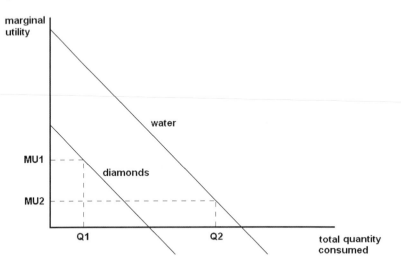

Figure 3.1   Water diamond paradox explained with marginal utility theory

Note the importance in this analysis of assuming that agents are capable of clearly recognizing which course of action best satisfies them and then selecting it. If this were not true, then this analysis may show how people should act, but not necessarily how they do act (that is, it would be prescriptive but not descriptive). However, another core concept in Neoclassicism is that agents are "rational," by which they mean that people are, indeed, able to recognize and choose the best option. This is a major theme throughout their work.

Marginal analysis was applied to a number of areas in economics including but not limited to firm behavior, consumer behavior, and price theory. It is noteworthy that during this period, economists were largely discussing these issues among themselves. This is not to say that there was not some participation from those in business and government, but this was diminishing as compared to during the Classical period. As economics became an academic discipline unto itself, the primary audience became other economists. This was one of but not the only reason for the shift from policy to more abstract and technical subjects.

Another significant development during this period was general equilibrium analysis. First explored by Marginalist Leon Walras, it is a framework in which all variables are mutually dependent, remain at rest until exogenous forces create a disturbance, and exist in a timeless world. What this means is that economic systems seek resting points in the same way that objects do in Newtonian physics. The standard supply and demand diagram illustrates just such a situation. Once we are at the equilibrium price and quantity, nothing will ever change again unless we shift one of the curves. Furthermore, the variables in a general equilibrium model are mutually dependent. To borrow an analogy from Alfred Marshall, imagine three balls resting in a bowl – removing any one (which is akin to an exogenous force) will cause the other two to move in response. However, they will quickly achieve a new equilibrium position and remain there until another ball is removed or added. Extending this concept to the economy, the idea is that all prices and quantities in every market are dependent upon each other and that a single equilibrium position exists among them. Moving one price or quantity necessitates the adjustment of the others. Last, this is a timeless analysis because if one were shown a series of photographs of the bowl with various numbers of balls in it, it would be impossible to determine which happened first, second, third, and so on (assuming one can both add and subtract balls). In this approach, the past has no qualitative effect on the future. Strictly speaking, time does not matter in the sense that there is no logical order to a set of equilibrium points.

Generally speaking, the Marginalists approached questions of economic theory with the belief that they were describing natural, rather than social, behavior. This can be traced back to the Classical economists and Adam Smith, whose work emerged during a part of the Enlightenment when scholars were focusing on explaining what they thought to be natural human rights and proclivities. Hence, these economists saw themselves as offering universal principles of economic behavior, not simply those of nineteenth-century western Europeans. In addition, they had a strong preference for a priori theorizing. To understand what this means, consider the structure of an argument. It consists of a series of premises that lead to a conclusion. For example:

Premise 1: All economists are risk-averse.
Premise 2: Susan is an economist.
Therefore: Susan is risk-averse.

Two important properties of arguments are validity and cogency. The former requires that the conclusion is supported by the premises. This is clearly true above. If all economists are risk-averse and Susan is an economist, then she, too, must be risk-averse. Cogency, however, requires both validity and that the premises be warranted. Thus, we must also know if "all economists are risk averse" and "Susan is an economist" are reasonable statements. Unfortunately, while determining validity is a relatively objective process, "warranted" is more subjective. This is particularly true when we are talking about modeling complex phenomena where it is absolutely necessary to simplify the object of our study. Is saying that firms are short-term profit maximizers a fatal over-simplification or close enough for present purposes? This is a difficult question to resolve, especially because the answer could be "yes" in one context and "no" in another, even within the same school of thought, depending on the goal and scope of the study in question. No wonder economists disagree!

One of the issues in considering whether or not premises are warranted is a philosophical or methodological one: what is the proper means of developing premises? In terms of the argument above, is it more reliable to conduct empirical research to discover economists' attitude toward risk (via survey or controlled experiments, for example), or is it actually more reliable to rely on one's own abstract reasoning and intuition, as in "It seems logical to me that economists would be risk-averse?" The Marginalists inherited from the Classicals the belief that it was the latter (Prasch 1996). Their argument, based on Scottish Common Sense philosophy, was that it was too easy for a researcher to bias premises derived from observation because the latter is strongly affected by what we expect to see. The world is not full of facts waiting for us to discover them. Rather, we build science on our interpretations of data, interpretations inevitably affected by our preconceptions. Hence, you may end up inadvertently "proving" whatever you thought was suspected in the first place. For that reason, the Marginalists argued, we should build premises based on introspection and make them so self-evident as to be beyond question. This requires that we build economic arguments by starting with axiomatic first principles (a priori premises) based on abstract reasoning rather than observation.

THE RISE TO PROMINENCE OF MODERN NEOCLASSICISM

At the core of modern Neoclassical theory are marginal analysis, the rationality assumption, general equilibrium modeling, and a priori-ism. However, this school of thought is so large and varied that it is impossible to point at a single set of contemporary theories associated with these ideas. Indeed, the range is such that there are acrimonious fights within Neoclassicism and between subgroups that would vehemently deny being members of the same school of thought (Neoclassical Keynesians and Monetarists, for example). Nevertheless, because these disagreements are a question of the means of application of a common set of principles rather than a rejection of them, they will all be treated as Neoclassical here.

Neoclassicism did not always enjoy the monopoly it does now. This did not emerge until after the Second World War (Rutherford 2011; much of the following is based on his interpretation). Before that, Institutionalists, Austrians, and those who would later be called Post Keynesians were active participants along with Neoclassicals in "mainstream" economic discussions. A number of things occurred to change this situation and, in the process, the nature of Neoclassicism evolved too. The importance of these events goes well beyond this chapter, of course, and relates to the very *raison d'être* of this book. The key question is, did Neoclassicism become dominant because economists carefully considered all the alternatives and found it to offer superior explanations of the phenomena we study? If so, this volume is unnecessary. If not, then perhaps the relegation of non-Neoclassical theory to history of economic thought class has been premature.

The first important event that took place was related to the utility of many Neoclassical tools during the Second World War. Marginal analysis proved to be very useful in solving allocation and maximization problems under the conditions of full employment that the conflict created in the United States. To understand this, take the production possibility frontier shown in Figure 3.2. This diagram can be used to illustrate the social costs of allocating scarce resources to various types of production. Labeled on each axis is a particular good that could be produced using available resources (in this case, automobiles or rice). Combinations outside the curve are impossible to achieve because we have insufficient resources to do so, those inside the curve represent inefficient choices because they leave resources idle, and those on the perimeter are efficient choices because they employ all available resources.

It is assumed that economies will come to rest somewhere on the curve (more on why they believe this is true later), the choice of the exact position being the open question. Meanwhile, the production possibility frontier analysis defines the tradeoffs they face in making their selection. These are expressed in terms of opportunity costs, or what must be foregone in terms of the other good. This is consistent with their overall approach, measured at the margin. For example, say that we are currently at point C, but want to build one more car. The slope of the line shows how much rice must be sacrificed to do this (technically speaking, the slope of a line tangent to point C). Note that this varies along the curve, with the opportunity cost of automobiles rising as we produce more and more of them (that is, as we move up and to the left). This is because resources are not equally suited to each type of production. Rice is easier to grow in wet, swampy climates, while you need to build an automobile factory on dry, solid ground. As we first shift toward cars, then we take out of rice production resources that were more poorly suited to making the latter in the first place (that is, drier land). Hence, the cost is relatively low. But, if we continue on this course, we eventually end up using labor, capital, raw materials, and so on that would have been better used for making rice (wet, swampy land that will now need to be drained). The cost becomes very high.

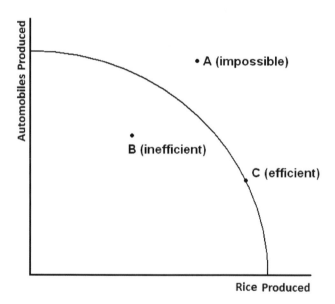

Figure 3.2   Production possibility frontier

Note that in order for costs to be measured in this way, we must be on the curve itself. We cannot be beyond it, of course, because that is impossible, and inside the perimeter one can have more of one good without giving up any of the other. Opportunity costs would not exist. And therein lies a key issue. This tool, designed to offer insights regarding tradeoffs under full employment, is not very useful outside that context – and the Great Depression was well outside. The problem during the 1930s was not the allocation of scarce resources, but the desperate need to find employment for an abundant one: labor. So long as there were unemployed citizens willing to work at the current wage rate, we were at a point analogous to B and could produce more without giving anything up. The marginal analysis of Neoclassicism does not help with this. And while it may be possible to look back and identify economists (inside and outside Neoclassicism) who offered useful contemporary analyses, in general the reputation of our profession suffered from its apparent inability to explain the greatest crisis capitalism has ever faced.

It was therefore all the more striking when, in the full employment environment of the Second World War, tools based on the same concepts as illustrated in the production possibility frontier were employed with great success and in contexts well beyond the economy. War production pushed the United States to the perimeter and suddenly opportunity costs were terribly important. Particularly in contrast to the struggles economists faced in trying to end the Depression, this had the effect of raising the prestige of Neoclassical economics. It was well placed to offer practical advice in the 1940s.

A second factor that affected the popularity and development of Neoclassical economics was the Cold War antagonism toward any analysis that did not argue that capitalism was best. Tensions were very high in what was perceived to be a life-or-death struggle with the Soviet Union and the People's Republic of China. Economics professors (among others) thought to be sympathetic to enemies of Western Democracy could face serious sanctions from their university, funding agencies, the government, private sector interests, and so on. This created an atmosphere that favored schools of thought whose analyses were more inclined to suggest that market solutions were best. While Neoclassicism certainly did not blindly support capitalism, its conclusions were generally more friendly to free markets than those of Institutionalism and followers of Keynes (and certainly Marxism!). Hence, this meant that the Neoclassical economists were favored in hiring, promotion, funding, and so on. In addition, because there was little to be gained from inviting the scrutiny of those searching for subversives, economists of all varieties (including Neoclassicals) had an incentive to make their work less accessible to those outside of the discipline. Economic research became less policy-oriented and instead more mathematical, abstract, and theoretical. So while the success of the technical tools used during the Second World War and the continued professionalization of the discipline no doubt played a role, the external pressures created by the social and political forces described here were decisive. These served not only to muffle several voices that had been active in the pre-war scholarly debate, but created a strong us-versus-them environment in which issues were viewed in black and white and everyone was seen as either a good guy or a bad guy. It was also in this atmosphere that the conceptual distinction between so-called fact-based positive economics and opinion-based normative economics became popular. "Good" economists preferred the former and left the latter to the public or politicians or for their own more speculative and simplistic popular writings. Venturing into normative economics was permitted, but potentially dangerous as it left you open to politically based attacks and was viewed as less scientific. Hence the popularity of framing your research as "positive."

Neoclassicism thus emerged from this period as the dominant paradigm. Note that this discussion is not meant to be an indictment of that school of thought, however. One of the core themes of this book is that there are interesting and useful concepts to be found in every approach (not to be confused with the idea that they are all correct). What I do mean to point out, though, is that there was no discipline-wide debate that left Neoclassicism the winner, nor was there an insidious plot by Neoclassicals to take over economics and intentionally reduce the roles played by other schools of thought. Rather, economics is a subculture embedded within a larger culture, and pressures from the latter were decisive in creating the situation that exists today. And unfortunately, at least from the perspective of this book, the collapse of the Soviet Union did not reverse this process and return us to a point of open exchange among diverse, scientific positions (although movements supporting such an outcome do exist and appear to be gaining some momentum). Instead, once established, Neoclassicism's monopoly position created numerous barriers to alternate approaches that did not fall along with the Berlin Wall.

One of the most important residual barriers to pluralism is that related to publication. Recall the discussion from Chapter two regarding the means by which economists are trained, promoted, and rewarded. Central to the last two is the journal system wherein rankings play a key role in determining the credit a professor earns for a particular publication. As a result of the events discussed above, the list that we inherited from the twentieth century puts Neoclassical journals squarely at the top, indeed, on essentially the entire list. The reward system thus continues to be heavily weighted against those pursuing other approaches. As a consequence, they are often relegated to smaller institutions where research is not as highly valued and the opportunity to train PhDs is extremely limited. This both retards the further development of the school of thought in question and creates a significant obstacle to the training of new generations of like-minded economists. The situation is such that, generally speaking, most economists are rarely aware that communities of scholars outside of Neoclassicism even exist. A major purpose of this book is to help reverse this trend.

MODERN NEOCLASSICAL THEORY (AND THE FULL EMPLOYMENT ASSUMPTION)

Modern Neoclassical economists, like the Marginalists, tend to focus their studies on the behavior of the individual. It is their belief that economics done properly starts at the level of the representative agent. This is so because social forces are seen as, if not totally unimportant, at least secondary. Economic behavior is law-like and universal in the sense that a model that applies to twenty-first-century Germans also explains (with perhaps minor modifications) twenty-first-century Koreans, twentieth-century Chileans, second-century Romans, and so on. It is in that sense akin to human physiology. If we know how humans digest food today, then we know how they digest food everywhere across time and space. Examinations of history and institutions are of only minor interest.

Such an approach puts microeconomics at the core of the Neoclassical research agenda, for it is this level at which they believe behavior truly reveals itself.[1] Hence, macroeconomics should have "microfoundations," or a clear exposition of how individuals in the model behave. As has already been explained, they view economic agents as being rational, self-interested, and focused on making decisions at the margin. What has not been mentioned so far is that Neoclassicals do not believe that it is strictly necessary for people to actually be rational, self-interested, and decision makers at the margin, only that they act as if they were rational, self-interested, and decision makers at the margin. This as-if method is important and shows up at a number of levels, for instance, in the methodological belief that it is more important to build models that accurately predict behavior than accurately describe it. Take the theory that businesses calculate marginal revenue and marginal cost curves in order to determine where to set their price (something you may have learned in a microeconomics class – no worries if you did not). In point of fact, it is very unlikely that they could do this even if they wanted to as the necessary information is rarely available. However, say Neoclassicals, assuming that this is what they do, even if it turns out they do not, nevertheless generates a model that accurately describes the real world.

On that basis, it is a useful model. A parallel would be making predictions under the assumption that Isaac Newton was correct that time and space are constants, even though modern physicists broadly reject that view in favor of Albert Einstein's relativity. Yet, for 99.9 percent of the phenomena we observe, Newtonian premises generate accurate predictions. It is more important that our assumptions create reliable forecasts than accurately reflect underlying behavior.

This position is consistent with the foundation in Scottish Common Sense philosophy mentioned earlier. If we develop first principles by asking managers how they set price or observing their behavior, then we are likely to contaminate our data with our own preconceptions. Your senses cannot be trusted. Better to begin by laying out premises based on our carefully considered, abstract reasoning, even if it generates assumptions that may otherwise seem questionable. Thus, the fact that the typical Neoclassical microeconomics class says very little about what actually happens in the day-to-day operations of a real-world business is not considered a weakness. Rather, it is a function of their view of the correct manner in which to understand economic behavior.

It was mentioned above that one of the primary foci of Neoclassical economics is constrained optimization, or choosing among alternatives in the face of tradeoffs. In the context of the production possibilities curve, when resources are already fully employed, what is the cost of shifting from one point to another? However, it was also suggested that if we are at less-than-full employment, opportunity costs do not exist and this type of analysis is no longer helpful.

Despite the obvious limitations this could create, Neoclassicals do not view it as a serious issue because they believe that the economy automatically tends toward full employment. This is true even of the more interventionist members of their school of thought. Take, for example, this quote from Christina Romer, one-time head of President Barack Obama's Council of Economic Advisors: "The prevailing view among economists is that there is a level of economic activity, often referred to as full employment, at which the economy could stay forever" (Romer 2008; by "economists" she means Neoclassical economists). Romer believes this despite the fact that she is one of those who would argue that we can and should help the economy if it falls below full employment. But we are only helping, it is fixing itself anyway. At the other end of the spectrum within Neoclassicism are those who not only believe this is true, but argue that any attempt by government policy makers to speed the process is doomed to failure. The economy works best when left alone.

In either event, however, the end result is still the same: full employ-ment is guaranteed, if not continually, then eventually. For this reason, Neoclassicals sometimes frame their analyses as being more appropriate to the long run than the short run. In other words, while we may be inside the production possibilities curve right now, we can nevertheless employ tools based on opportunity cost tradeoffs because eventually we will be back on the frontier. That is the natural position of the economy.

There is a variety of explanations of how self-correction occurs, each focusing on a different aspect of the process. The loanable funds theory of interest, for example, is sometimes employed and offers other insights into their view of the macroeconomy. Start with a simple economy wherein there is no government or foreign sector, only domestic firms and households. Say that Y represents total output. Note that it must also therefore equal total income and total expenditure. This is always true in a closed system because every time you make an expenditure, it is necessarily for something (that is, output) and it becomes someone else's income. For example, if you decide to get a $5 hamburger for lunch, you make a $5 expenditure for a $5 unit of output (the hamburger) and the vendor earns $5 in income. One transaction generates three identical values, which is why total expenditures necessarily equal total output which equals total income.

Further assume that only households earn income (that is, firms do not retain any profits) and that they either spend it on consumption (C) or they save it (S):

$$Y = C + S \tag{3.1}$$

Meanwhile, firms undertake physical investment, or additions to their ability to produce output (new factories, for example) and, since they have no income, they must borrow to do so. This means that in terms of expenditures, only two things are purchased in this simple economy: consumer goods (C) and investment goods (I):

$$Y = C + I \tag{3.2}$$

Note that it is unnecessary to take separate account of the raw materials the firms used to make the consumer and investment goods they sell because those costs are already included in the price of the final product. For instance, in the hamburger example above, the vendor already included the labor, hamburger meat, bun, lettuce, tomato, ketchup, and so on. The sale price is equal to those costs plus profit. If we valued national output by counting both the final price of the hamburger AND the raw materials, this would count the same values multiple times.

A very important conclusion from comparing Equations (3.1) and (3.2) is that it must be true that $I = S$. In other words, in equilibrium, total savings must equal total investment. That this is true under the assumptions made above is not controversial. There are, however, strong disagreements regarding the process by which the equality is maintained.

The loanable funds theory of interest argues that interest rates play the key role. In fact, not only do they keep $I = S$, but they are also what creates the strong tendency toward full employment. To understand this, first return to the household. How do they decide how much to spend versus save? In the Neoclassical framework, this is determined by the rate of interest (r). Households would rather, they assume, spend all their money on consumption goods today. The only thing that prevents them from doing so is the offer of interest from banks. The more banks offer, the more households will save for tomorrow:

$$S = f(r) \atop +$$
(3.3)

Meanwhile, a key determinant of firms' investment is also the current rate of interest, but, since they have no income and are forced to borrow to finance any projects, it has a negative impact:[2]

$$I = f(r) \atop -$$
(3.4)

Last, banks pay interest to households on S and earn it from firms on I.

Now consider the following scenario. Say we start at $S = I$ with the economy at full employment. What would happen if firms decided to reduce investment? This could potentially cause recession as spending declined and workers found themselves unemployed. However, while this may occur as the economy adjusts, it does not represent the new equilibrium position. This is so because a problem has been created for banks: they are still paying interest on the same volume of saving, but the fall in firm borrowing to invest means that their revenues have declined. They now have unborrowed savings in their vaults. They can address this, though, by lowering interest rates. According to Equations (3.1) and (3.2), this will have the effect of reducing S while raising I. How much will they lower the interest rate? Enough to ensure that all savings are once again borrowed, which occurs at $S = I$.

This, then, is the process by which the equality of S and I is maintained. But there is more. Say that we had started at $S = I = \$500$

and that the initial decline in I left it at $400. As banks lowered r in response, I would start to rise back above $400 and S would fall below $500. For the sake of argument, say that the new equilibrium is $S = I = $450. The net fall in investment was therefore $50, and so overall demand declined by that amount. This would leave us at less-than-full employment. However, if savings also fell by $50, this means that consumption must have risen by the same amount: the net fall in investment is exactly offset by the rise in consumption. When modeled more formally it can be shown that this is precisely what happens in every scenario, leading to the general conclusion that whenever demand falls and threatens recession, interest rates will adjust in a manner that reinvigorates spending just enough to keep us at full employment.[3]

This is the manner by which the economy automatically self-corrects to return us to full employment, thereby allowing the use of opportunity cost-based analyses. Interest rates are, incidentally, viewed as important variables in the macroeconomy in general and not just in this context. It is seen as a common culprit in the onset of recession, for example, wherein monetary policy may drive interest rates too high and cause a fall in investment and overall spending. Rudiger Dornbusch writes that "None of the U.S. expansions of the last 40 years died in bed of old age; every one was murdered by the Federal Reserve" (quoted in Temin 1998, p. 37). And a common recommendation among Neoclassicals is that nations should increase their savings rates. This is so because this would cause $S > I$, which encourages banks to lower r and thereby encourage I. While this would not cause a change in overall employment, since it just means moving from one full employment position to another, it would nevertheless raise long-term growth as the higher level of investment would raise productivity in the future.

The above gives a small taste of modern Neoclassical economics, but it is a very large school of thought with many variations. Still, these are variations on a common theme, wherein rationality, decision making on the margin, opportunity costs, and the full employment assumption all play an important role. Neoclassicism absolutely dominates the discipline both in North America and throughout the rest of the world and one cannot understand how economics works or schools of thought evolve without understanding it.

METHOD

Because it was central to the story above, a great deal about method has already been said. But, to summarize, Neoclassicals believe that the logical focal point of economic analysis is the individual. In modeling their behavior, one should endeavor to formulate axiomatic (that is, self-evident) premises derived from reflection and abstract reasoning rather than observation. In addition, phenomena are usually placed within an equilibrium framework and analyses focus on the marginal unit. Last, the as-if method is perfectly acceptable and the propriety of a model is based more on its predictive than descriptive abilities.

VIEWS OF HUMAN NATURE AND JUSTICE

Humans, as suggested above, are viewed as individualistic, at least with respect to the subject of our discipline. Religion, kinship patterns, language, and so on may vary from culture to culture, but economic behavior is universal. Neoclassicals believe that one of our tasks as economists is to identify those laws. Adam Smith said, for example, that humans naturally want to truck, barter, and trade and that they are self-interested. This is not meant as a description of eighteenth-century Scots, but of all people everywhere and throughout history. In terms of justice, Neoclassicals believe that the goal of policy should be to ensure consumer sovereignty in the market. What this means is that they want consumers to be the ones who are really in charge of what gets produced. On the surface, it may appear as if firms are making those decisions; but in a truly competitive market they are simply reacting to customers' demands. Thus, the consumers are the sovereigns. Neoclassicals also believe that the profits and wages earned in a competitive market are objective reflections of the true value of those agents' contributions. Any income disparities, regardless of size, are not only fair, but they are to be encouraged since these were ultimately created not by the individuals in question, but consumers. Redistributing income would only serve to skew production away from consumer preferences.

STANDARDS

Primary

In discussing primary standards of behavior, one must first be careful to distinguish between Neoclassical and mainstream. The latter is a broader term, including some non-Neoclassical approaches that have gained a measure of acceptance. That said, most mainstream economics is still Neoclassical.

One of the core concepts in the latter is the rationality of individuals. This is taken to be axiomatic. Of course people know what will please them most and of course they will select the courses of action that lead to these outcomes. In addition, these preferences are internal and independent of those of others. All this is consistent with the belief that economic behavior in general is natural, not cultural. Humans are also assumed to be instinctively drawn toward market-based solutions.

This rooting of the basics of economic behavior in the individual means that even macro theories in Neoclassicism must have microfoundations. Another primary standard is the assumption that economic processes tend toward equilibrium. In this context, the specific resting point toward which macroeconomies automatically move is one consistent with full employment. There are Neoclassical models that allow for less-than-full employment, but they do so by assuming some friction or interference with the market process. Otherwise, as indicated in the Christine Romer quote above, they believe we would stay at full employment forever.

Secondary

On the other hand, while Neoclassicals mistrust observational data like surveys, this is not a hard and fast rule as these have been employed extensively in exchange rate research where their traditional methods have had difficulty. Still, one is expected to offer a justification. In addition, research focusing on specific nations or cultures is not typical because economic behavior is seen as natural. But it is generally acceptable if an argument can be made that is consistent with the underlying theory. In fact, this is true of a wide variety of subjects that might not otherwise be considered economics, per se. If elements of the traditional economic model can be applied, then the topic is fair game. Likewise, while government intervention is generally viewed as undesirable, if it can be shown that there are unavoidable frictions or that market failure (a situation in which the market is unable to supply a good in the quantity that society would otherwise desire; education is often used as an example) exists, then it is justifiable.

CONTEMPORARY ACTIVITIES

As Neoclassicism is the dominant school of thought, it would almost be easier to point out which journals, associations, and conferences were not organized by them. In the United States, the primary organization is the

American Economics Association. Founded in 1885, their web page lists its stated purposes as:

1.   The encouragement of economic research, especially the historical and statistical study of the actual conditions of industrial life.
2.   The issue of publications on economic subjects.
3.   The encouragement of perfect freedom of economic discussion. The Association as such will take no partisan attitude, nor will it commit its members to any position on practical economic questions.

It holds one major conference every year in early January, timed to fall between the fall and spring semesters of most universities. The meeting is important beyond the papers being presented and the social gatherings hosted for it is also the focal point of the job market for PhD economists. Employers, especially but not exclusively academic ones, submit information to *Job Openings for Economists*, an American Economics Association publication. Well before the conference, candidates, often soon to be brand-new PhDs, search this document for positions that match their qualifications. They submit the requested materials and hope that they are contacted. Meanwhile, employers sift through what is often very many curriculum vitae, research papers, and so on and prepare a list of potential employees to interview. As suggested above, the latter takes place at the annual convention. Favorite candidates are typically invited to campus for more in-depth interviewing.

I mention all this to emphasize the critical importance of this conference. The overwhelming majority of universities hire new faculty via this process. In addition, universities have limited travel money. Therefore, an Austrian economist hoping to attend the Austrian Economics Research Conference might be forced to instead spend travel money to go to the American Economics Association meetings in order to participate in the interviewing. Some schools of thought are lucky in that the American Economics Association meetings also include sessions from their perspective, but these are invariably a side show and the space allotted to these has been reduced over the years. The point here is that this represents yet another obstacle to a pluralistic approach to economics. It is very difficult for other schools of thought to grow and prosper. This is not, to repeat a point made above, an indictment of Neoclassicism, per se. Had any school of thought ended up in such a monopolistic position it would have created an environment like this.

CRITICISMS

It is difficult to summarize the objections to Neoclassicism because they come from so many directions. As it is the primary school of thought in economics, every other one feels an obligation to outline what they see as its shortcomings as part of the justification for their own existence.

But a Marxist critique of Neoclassicism would be very different from that of a Post Keynesian or an Austrian. A listing would therefore be pointless, not to mention confusing given that those schools of thought, themselves, are not explained until subsequent chapters. However, one point about which each would agree is that they feel blocked out of the conversation. As suggested above, Neoclassicism is dominant in graduate programs, journal rankings, textbooks, conferences, and in policy circles. It is one thing, say those coming from alternate perspectives, for the mainstream to disagree with them; it is another to be prevented from participating.

One general criticism from several schools of thought is directed at the priori/as-if method. How, they ask, is abstract reasoning and reflection more unbiased than observation, especially when one is free to posit as-if premises that are not intended to even approximate real-world behavior? In fact, the result might be just the opposite since one lacks an anchor like the real world (which is a perfect model of itself) against which premises must be checked. The a priori/as-if method can lead to situations in which the researcher is creating premises, consciously or not, designed to support a preconceived conclusion like full employment or market efficiency.

Of course, Neoclassicals say that they do compare their models to the real world, but only in terms of predictions. It does not matter how unrealistic assumptions are, they argue, so long as the theory generates accurate forecasts. Critics respond, however, that while this might be a defensible approach were it actually followed, it is not. Neoclassical research almost never does this, preferring instead abstract mathematical modeling as sufficiently persuasive. In reality, there is no systematic process by which these are vetted and so methods that claim to be designed to prevent uncontrolled speculation actually generate exactly that (but with a veneer of respectability created by pretentious mathematical symbols).

FINAL REJOINDER

It should first be pointed out that Neoclassical economists are not necessarily aware of these criticisms. To be so would require that there be more communication between them and other schools of thought than actually exists. And, as the mainstream, they do not need to engage other approaches.

That said, the most obvious response is that were their approach not superior, it would not be the mainstream. Indeed, as indicated at the beginning of this chapter, they dominate every aspect of the discipline, from all levels of education through policy. In the marketplace of ideas, they see themselves as having outcompeted everyone else. That others claim that their perspective is suppressed is simply petulance. If you have a better idea, they argue, then let us hear it. We all have the same goal: to better understand the economy. The fact that Neoclassicism is on top should be sufficient evidence that abstract mathematical modeling based on axiomatic assumptions and the as-if method are extremely effective.

FURTHER READING

Suggesting further reading for those interested in knowing more about Neoclassicism is a bit difficult since this school of thought is so large and has such a wide variety of subareas. In addition, because they are the dominant paradigm, those writing from this perspective are unlikely to identify themselves as Neoclassicals and write simply as "economists." Because of this, it would generally be safe to assume that, unless otherwise stated, a given publication comes from this perspective.

More specifically, just about any textbook on the market today is written from the Neoclassical perspective. This includes not just micro- and macroeconomics, but labor, international trade, game theory, exchange rates, development, economic history, public finance, money and banking, and so on. In addition, economic commentators, even if they appear to strongly disagree with one another, are almost exclusively Neoclassical. See, for example, the blogs authored by Paul Krugman, Greg Mankiw, and Robert Reich in http://krugman.blogs.nytimes.com/, http://gregmankiw.blogspot.com/ and http://robertreich.org/, respectively. That these encompass what would be generally categorized as both liberal and conservative view points is a testament to the size and range of Neoclassicism. But they are nevertheless drawing on the same basic set of tools and analyses to understand the economy.

Also worth investigating is the popular *Freakonomics* book by Steven Levitt and Stephen Dubner (2005), which applies basic Neoclassical concepts to erstwhile non-economic topics. A similar book that was actually published much earlier was Steven Landsburg's *The Armchair Economist* (1993). Tim Harford's *The Undercover Economist* (2006) and Charles Wheelan and Burton Malkiel's *Naked Economics* (2010) also represent easy-to-read applications and explanations of Neoclassical economics.

NOTES

1. Note that the very idea that there is a distinction between micro- and macroeconomics is not necessarily shared by other schools of thought. Those believing that human behavior is essentially social, for example, argue that it is misleading and meaningless to draw such a distinction.
2. Students often ask if r is meant to represent the same rate of interest for both the households and firms. No, it is not. Obviously, if banks are to earn a profit, they must charge more to firms than they pay to households. But we do not bother to differentiate because we are only concerned with movements in these variables, not their actual levels, and they would almost certainly move together. If, for example, banks are forced to pay households more to get their savings, then this raises their costs and they will charge firms more for borrowing.
3. Starting the analysis by lowering S instead of I, incidentally, gives the same result.

REFERENCES

Harford, T. (2006), *The Undercover Economist: Exposing Why the Rich Are Rich, the Poor Are Poor – and Why You Can Never Buy a Decent Used Car!* Oxford: Oxford University Press.

Landsburg, S.E. (1993), *The Armchair Economist: Economics and Everyday Life*, New York: Free Press.

Levitt, S.D. and S.J. Dubner (2005), *Freakonomics: A Rogue Economist Explores the Hidden Side of Everything*, New York: William Morrow.

Prasch, R.E. (1996), "The origins of the a priori method in classical political economy: a reinterpretation," *Journal of Economic Issues*, **30** (4), 1105–25.

Romer, C.D. (2008), "Business cycles," in D.R. Henderson (ed.), *The Concise Encyclopedia of Economics*, Indianapolis, IN: Liberty Fund, available at http://www.econlib.org/library/Enc/BusinessCycles.html (accessed July 26, 2010).

Rutherford, M. (2011), *The Institutionalist Movement in American Economics, 1918–1947: Science and Social Control*, Cambridge: Cambridge University Press.

Smith, A. (1776), *An Inquiry into the Nature and Causes of the Wealth of Nations*, London: W. Strahan and T. Cadell, reprinted in 2004, Amazon Digital Services, Inc., Digireads.com.

Temin, P. (1998), "The causes of American business cycles: an essay in economic historiography," in J.C. Fuhrer and S. Schuh (eds), *Beyond Shocks: What Causes Business Cycles?* Boston, MA: Federal Reserve Bank of Boston, pp. 37–59.

Wheelan, C.J. and B.G. Malkiel (2010), *Naked Economics: Undressing the Dismal Science*, New York: W.W. Norton.

4. Marxism

No other non-mainstream school of thought has had a more prominent role in economic policy, scholarly discourse, and world politics than Marxism. It has been the subject of continuous and acrimonious debate, with detractors blaming it for untold death and misery and supporters pointing to capitalism as the true villain. Complicating matters is the fact that a great many things pass for "Marxism." Because of its high profile and obvious anti-establishment bent, [it is an attractive destination for anyone dissatisfied with the mainstream] regardless of their affinity for or knowledge of his work. Thus, some Marxists are truly Marx scholars, others have adopted some aspects of his analysis without the overall framework, and still more are essentially left-leaning individuals who like what the label communicates. Even those in the first group are hardly homogeneous given that interpretations of Marx's massive volume of work can vary significantly. On top of all this, there are economists whose research draws heavily on *Capital*, *The Communist Manifesto*, and so on, but who do not consider themselves Marxists!

Although this makes it impossible to identify a single, modern Marxist perspective, the starting point of this chapter must still obviously be Marx himself. It was his writings, his theories, and his analyses that provided the catalyst for what followed. After his work is explained some modern variants can be examined.

FOUNDATIONS OF MARX'S ECONOMICS: HEGEL, CLASSICAL ECONOMICS, AND SOCIALISM

Karl Marx was born in Prussia in 1818. He came from a middle-class family and his father was a well-respected lawyer (a convert, for political reasons, from Judaism to Lutheranism). Marx studied at several universities, including Jena where he took his PhD. It was during his undergraduate studies at the University of Berlin, however, that he came under the influence of a philosopher whose work would have a major impact on his thinking: Georg Friedrich Wilhelm Hegel (1770–1831). The latter believed that concepts evolved, both slowly and by discrete, revolutionary

leaps, from incompleteness toward rationality and concreteness. Figure
4.1 offers a visual representation of his theory. The basic idea is that
phenomena in their early form, while they may at first seem satisfactory,
eventually prove to be less solid than believed (and therefore "abstract").
This leads to negation, or the process of laying bare the incompleteness
and flaws and addressing them. What emerges is something more
concrete and useful. However, it may itself prove to be incomplete or
flawed and thus also be revealed to be abstract, requiring another round
of negation, and so on. Over time, the incomplete and flawed becomes
increasingly complete and rational.

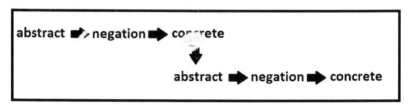

Figure 4.1   The Hegelian dialectic

Applying his philosophy to history, Hegel believed that we were moving
society from imperfect, self-denying systems like slavery to more complete ones based on rationality, constitutional rights, and freedom. Each
period operates smoothly at first, but contradictions emerge as the
incompleteness of that stage becomes obvious. [The process of negation
attempts to preserve aspects that were useful and eliminate and reform
those that were not.] Hegel further believed that the driving force
underlying this process was the development of our collective consciousness over time. As this shared rationality evolves, so we change our
material world to become consistent with it. In this sense, the great
figures of the past are acting as the conduit for our broader social
consciousness, which he called the Geist or Spirit. Hegel believed we
were inevitably moving toward a secular state wherein rationality and
freedom are valued above all (note that within this context he did not see
the existence of a strong state apparatus as being at odds with the
existence of individual freedom).

   While the existence of such a teleological dialectical process became a
cornerstone of Marx's economic analysis, he disagreed strongly with
Hegel's characterization of the driving force. In Hegel's view, ideas
changed reality. The Geist guided prevailing social philosophies, which
then led people to enact political and economic change. Instead, Marx
believed that reality changed ideas. There is, he thought, a natural and

inevitable sequence to the evolution of economic systems and this occurs independently of our philosophies: slave-based societies lead to feudalism, which leads to capitalism, which leads to socialism, which leads to communism.[1] This is the dominant process and we do not control it, it controls us.

For Marx, to a large extent, world views change only after the fact and simply to justify the social relations of production that already exist under the new economic system. This is the manner in which reality changes ideas. Consider feudalism. Within the manor system, there were lords (with various ranks therein) and serfs. The former owned land and maintained an armed force, while the latter farmed and owed a portion of subsequent output to the lord of the manor. In exchange for this, they received protection from the cruel world around them. There were social, political, and religious justifications for these social relations, such as the divine right of kings. In Marx's eyes, however, these arose as a result of the development of this new stage of history, they did not cause it. Feudalism was the inevitable consequence of the collapse of the slave-based system that had existed under the Roman empire. It flatters us to think that we effected this change, but the truth is somewhat different.

Marx's perspective was also influenced by the abuses that accompanied the Industrial Revolution. While it is true that life under feudalism was hardly ideal for the underclass and though it can be argued (as even Marx did) that the Industrial Revolution brought with it a massive increase in productivity and technology, the fruits thereof were hardly shared equally. Conditions for the propertyless class were often abysmal, the work mind-numbing, and the wages barely above subsistence. This brought negative reactions from a variety of sources – political, literary, religious, social, and economic – and modern socialism emerged as a direct result of this Dickensian environment.

Not only did Marx share these concerns, but he thought that capitalism did serious psychological damage to the worker. People should, he believed, have the power to control their own destinies. They should be free to choose what they produce, to determine how that product will be used, to cooperate with (rather than compete against) their fellow workers, and to decide what skills they would like to develop. But under capitalism, workers are forced to submit to the will of those who own the means of production. They lose control of their fate and actually become cogs in the machinery of their own exploitation. This makes them more than just de facto slaves. Because of the conditions created by capitalism, Marx says workers are alienated (or separated) from their humanity. They cannot be free or achieve their true potential. Capitalism thus subjects workers to conditions that are objectionable from both a physical and psychological standpoint.

While some socialists believed that reforms from within were possible, Marx thought that the only solution was the total and absolute destruction of the system responsible for so much misery. Note how well this would fit into the framework suggested by the dialectic. Capitalism might simply be a stage of history, one whose imperfections are a function of the dysfunctional class relations it creates. While superior to feudalism, contradictions reveal themselves and lead to a process of negation that brings about a new, more advanced stage: socialism. In its time, this undergoes a similar transformation until communism emerges. And if the sequence is supposed to bring us toward increasing rationality and justice, then our final chapter might well be a happy one wherein economic injustice has been eliminated. Such is the world represented by communism. Class conflict will disappear and people will no longer be forced to serve the capitalist by undertaking the same demeaning, dreary jobs, day in and day out. We will finally be at peace and able to lead rich, fulfilling lives.

Although Marx does have some thoughts to offer regarding socialism and communism, the overwhelming majority of his writing is devoted to understanding capitalism and its contradictions. In pursuit of this, he made a serious study of the work of the Classical economists, including Adam Smith (1723–1790) and David Ricardo (1772–1823). Students (including me some years ago!) are generally surprised to discover that Marx employed the work of these early proponents of free markets. They had an important impact on, for example, Marx's exploitation theory. While it was obvious in the nineteenth century that the working classes were extremely poor, Marx was led to ask why: precisely, scientifically, and in the context of that stage of history. As a scholar, he was not satisfied with casual empiricism. What is it in the character of capitalism that creates these conditions? His answer was based on the labor theory of value developed by the Classical economists. Recall from the previous chapter that among the questions that interested them (and later the Neoclassicals) was what determined the value of a good. The answer suggested by the labor theory of value was that, in simple terms, it was a function of the physical exertion necessary to produce it. Everything else being equal, an object that required eight hours to manufacture was worth twice as much as one that required four. If a tool had been used in the process, its contribution in labor terms could be imputed.

Now consider the following. There are two classes in capitalism: capitalists, who own the means of production (that is, the physical and natural resources necessary to produce goods and services) and workers, who own the ability to undertake labor. The proceeds of any sales of goods and services are ultimately divided between the wages paid to workers and the profits retained by capitalists. However, if the labor theory of value is correct, then the latter can only exist if workers are not paid for the full amount of value they created. Ownership of the means of production does not create any value whatsoever, only the act of labor does. Note that this does not require that the capitalists be mean or greedy (though they may be). Any social system wherein a single class of people is permitted to own the only means of feeding, clothing, and otherwise meeting the needs of humanity will inevitably create such disparities and inequities. And the propertyless class has no choice but to submit.

Marx is not arguing that this is unfair, per se. Justice is a function of the stage of history in question and is thus relative. Under capitalism, capitalists are entitled to surplus labor and they may dispose of this as they wish. As he wrote in Volume one of *Capital*, "The surplus-value is his property; it has never belonged to anyone else" (Marx 1867 [1977], p. 732). However, just because something is legally and morally sanctioned does not mean it is beneficial. One of the premises of Hegel's dialectic is that history moves from imperfection and irrationality toward increasing completeness and rationality. The implication of this general rule is that the transformation toward communism is not a question of moving toward justice, but reasonableness and personal freedom. Slavery was "fair," feudalism was "fair," and capitalism is "fair." They are each, however, incomplete and will be witness to the emergence of contradictions that will be addressed during negation.

MARX AND THE END OF CAPITALISM

The historical dialectic and exploitation theory that he uses to explain the abuses of the Industrial Revolution are parts of a far more comprehensive examination of capitalism in motion and of the internal contradictions that would arise. Initially, Marx believed that capitalism would be extremely successful, taking over an increasing number of tasks in society and advancing into every part of the globe. Art, for example, would no longer be driven by a desire for self-expression or social commentary, but by the need to earn profit. Farmers would farm for market and not for themselves. Everything would eventually be evaluated on the basis of its ability to generate sales. And this would spread from country to country until capitalism ruled the globe.[2] At the same time, we would experience rapid and unprecedented increases in productivity as new technologies are developed and employed.

But contradictions arise. Consider the impact of the rising technology that accompanies the growth of capitalism. As labor-saving techniques are developed, firms eagerly employ them in order to cut costs. This eventually creates a problem, however, as only workers can be exploited. Machines cannot be worked for ten hours and paid for five; people can. Hence, there is much greater potential for profit in labor-intensive processes. Business owners do not perceive this, however, and even if they did they would still be forced to adopt labor-saving techniques since to do otherwise would cede market share to competitors.

This seems counterintuitive as one would think that lowering costs would raise profits. But that assumes we are holding prices constant. In a competitive environment, firms will instead be forced to lower them. Hence, while the first firm to create some labor-saving technique may see an increase in its rate of profit, once everyone does so then it is possible that competition may lower prices sufficiently to actually cause a decline in the rate of profit. This is precisely what Marx says must logically occur given that the total amount of profit available to firms is limited by the volume of labor in existence (holding certain other factors constant). Spreading that same profit over the larger number of goods rising productivity would create logically means that profit rates necessarily fall. This creates an internal contradiction: as capitalism matures, there is a tendency for the average rate of profit to fall (Marx 1885 [1977], pp. 317–38). This raises obvious problems for the survival of capitalism.

Note that to be a significant factor, profit rates do not have to continue to fall indefinitely, only to the point that they are relatively low. In that case, the economy would be more susceptible to crisis since a larger number of firms would be on the verge of bankruptcy. In other words, "A fall in the average rate of profit will therefore have destabilizing effects that persist even if it stopped falling a long time ago" (Kliman 2012, p. 18). Meanwhile, the interaction of the credit market and physical investment creates cyclical instability. Capitalists need to borrow extensively to fund their operations and banks and other financial institutions are eager to oblige – sometimes too eager. At the bottom of a slump when pessimism still reigns, interest rates tend to be low given the relative lack of demand for loans. This helps spur the recovery. Once it is well underway and the economy is booming, interest rates may remain low as new suppliers of financial credit, including speculators, enter the market. However, they often do so with few to no real resources backing their activities (Marx 1894 [1977], p. 619). More than just risky undertakings, Marx also argues that one witnesses outright fraud during this boom period (Marx 1894 [1977], p. 621). Many Marxists view the recent Financial Crisis in just this light.

All this encourages overinvestment, with the consequence that in late expansion some capitalists discover that their wares will not sell for the prices they expected. They had been encouraged by the earlier low cost of financing (fueled, remember, by speculation and fraud) to invest in projects for which no market really existed. Bankruptcies follow as factory owners cannot repay loans and the impact of these defaults spreads throughout the economy. This causes recession, which only reverses itself once financial and non-financial capitalists have recovered sufficiently to begin expanding once more.

Marx expected the above cycle of expansion and recession to repeat over and over under capitalism. Furthermore, because of the tendency of the long-run rate of profit to decline, he expected that these crises would become increasingly severe, with business failures and unemployment reaching ever-higher peaks. Throughout this process, the gap between rich and poor would grow and industry would be monopolized by an ever-shrinking number of capitalists. Eventually, the workers, who had been inadvertently organized by the capitalists, would no longer be willing to accept their lot:

> Along with the constantly diminishing number of the magnates of capital, who usurp and monopolize all advantages of this process of transformation, grows the mass of misery, oppression, slavery, degradation, exploitation; but with this too grows the revolt of the working class, a class always increasing in numbers, and disciplined, united, organized by the very mechanism of the process of capitalist production itself. The monopoly of capital becomes a fetter upon the mode of production, which has sprung up and flourished along with, and under it. Centralization of the means of production and socialization of labour at last reach a point where they become incompatible with their capitalist integument. This integument is burst asunder. The knell of capitalist private property sounds. The expropriators are expropriated. (Marx 1867 [1977], p. 929)

Note, too, that he doubts that the capitalists will submit willingly. As he writes, "Force is the midwife of every old society which is pregnant with a new one" (Marx 1867 [1977], p. 916). The process of negation has resolved the internal contradictions of capitalism and the latter has evolved into a higher form of economic organization.

MARX AND POST-CAPITALIST SOCIETY

As suggested above, Marx does not write nearly as much about the subsequent stages of history, that is, socialism and communism, but we can say this. At first, many aspects of capitalism survive. For example, workers receive something akin to a wage that corresponds to the number of hours they worked (Marx says each worker gets a "certificate"; Marx 1959, p. 118). This can be used to claim a share of consumption goods matching that contribution. This is not unlike what they had done in the previous stage of history. But now they receive the whole of that amount because there is no longer a class of people who own means of production and retain surplus value for themselves. Factories, and so on, become public property, like military bases, the Houses of Parliament, or the pyramids at Giza. Meanwhile, the government, which had earlier existed solely as a mechanism of control for the capitalist class, is run by the workers. This is the dictatorship of the proletariat.

Unfortunately, inequities in wealth will remain in this stage because some workers will be more productive than others, some will be married, some will have children, and so on. This is because they are, in this early post-capitalist society, "regarded *only as workers*, and nothing more is seen in them, everything else being ignored" (Marx 1959, p. 119, emphasis in original). Their contribution is thus evaluated solely on that basis, in a manner similar to that under capitalism. Eventually, however, these remaining contradictions will be resolved and a more humane and rational society will result:

> In a higher phase of communist society, after the enslaving subordination of the individual to the division of labor, and therewith also the antithesis between mental and physical labor, has vanished; after labor has become not only a means of life but life's prime want; after the productive forces have also increased with the all-around development of the individual, and all the springs of co-operative wealth flow more abundantly – only then can the narrow horizon of bourgeois right be crossed in its entirety and society inscribe on its banners: "From each according to his ability, to each according to his needs!" (Marx 1959, p. 119)

People become whole, productive, and happy. This is in stark contrast to life under capitalism, where the worker suffered not only materially but psychologically from the fact that she was forced to be a nameless cog in the machine that exploited her. Choice and control had been stripped away by the necessity of submitting to those who owned the means of production. This is no longer true under communism. Plus, the tremendous level of productivity achieved at this point eliminates the need for the division of labor and the consequent restrictions on what skills we are free to develop. We are finally able to enjoy true freedom. And, because it existed only to coerce one class into doing the bidding of another, the government will whither away in the classless society.

MODERN MARXISM

As suggested in the opening paragraph, many things pass for Marxism. It remains a very popular alternative to capitalist ideologies and is studied, in one form or another, in many disciplines. There are Marxist economists, sociologists, political scientists, literary analysts, feminists, scientists, artists, historians, philosophers, anthropologists, geographers, writers, and so on.

Perhaps the most important early extension of Marx's work was made by Vladimir I. Lenin (1870–1924) in *Imperialism, the Latest Stage of Capitalism* (1917). Recall that as capitalism matures, firms are forced by competitive pressures to replace workers with machines. This eventually lowers their rate of profit, creating an incentive for owners to look elsewhere for surplus value. Because the developing world is a prime, untapped source of as-yet unexploited workers, they will be drawn there. The desires of the target nations in this respect are irrelevant, for at this stage of capitalism businesses have evolved into powerful monopolistic combinations including both financial and non-financial firms. Capitalists are even in a position to goad governments into going to war on their behalf. This is precisely how Lenin saw the First World War, that is, as a fight among imperialist powers each hoping to secure access to parts of the globe from which surplus value could be drained. Meanwhile, as the rate of exploitation may be quite high in the developing world given the lack of mechanization, capitalists can use some of the surplus to bribe their wealthier domestic workers (what Lenin called the "labor aristocracy"). In this way, the collapse of capitalism is delayed – but not prevented.

Such a theory had obvious appeal to the poverty-stricken and oppressed people in the developing world. However, because so many were in pre-industrial economies, Marx's placement of socialist revolution squarely in capitalist societies did not necessarily ring true to them. For this reason, the Maoist version of Marxism, developed by Chinese communist leader Mao Zedong, became popular. It argued that the rural peasantry (seen as analogous to the struggling 'third world' countries) was the true mechanism for socialist revolution, not the urban proletariat (seen as representative of the capitalist imperialist nations and their labor aristocracy). In addition, Mao was very explicit about the need for violence, especially guerrilla warfare, to resolve the contradictions that emerged under capitalism. Once accomplished, bourgeois values would continue to permeate society, requiring a second "cultural" revolution.

Changes also took place within traditional Marxism. It has been remarked by some adherents that, contrary to Marx's predictions, long-run rates of profit appear not to be falling but are, in fact, rising. If true, this is problematic since it is one of the internal contradictions that is supposed to help bring on crises capitalism. Paul Baran and Paul Sweezy (1966) developed a theory aimed at reconciling this alleged empirical inconsistency. Essentially, they argue that markets will not remain as competitive as Marx assumed. Now consider the impact of the rising levels of productivity that are supposed to occur as capitalism matures. These should lower the cost of production, just as Marx said. But in Baran and Sweezy's world, because firms are not forced to lower price in order to remain competitive, their rates of profit rise. This, they argue, matches what we observe in the real world.

This creates a potential problem, however, as the falling rate of profit was one of the forces that Marx said would contribute to the collapse of capitalism (since it would make firms more vulnerable during the cyclic crises that would occur). But Baran and Sweezy say that this is still problematic since rising rates of profit would mean an increasing portion of national income would go to the capitalists, whose consumption would not keep pace. For growth to continue, therefore, investment would have to compensate by accelerating at an accelerating rate. They argue that it will not:

> What this implies, however, is nonsensical from an economic standpoint. It means that a larger and larger volume of producer goods would have to be turned out for the sole purpose of producing a still larger and larger volume of producer goods in the future. Consumption would be a diminishing proportion of output, and the growth of the capital stock would have no relation to the actual or potential expansion of consumption. (Baran and Sweezy 1966, p. 81)

Roughly speaking, they are saying that continued growth would require that an increasing percentage of national income be devoted solely to machines that make other machines, not machines that make consumer goods. As they assume this to be a logical impossibility, they see this as a process that still leads to crisis.

Andrew Kliman, however, argues that not only is such a scenario quite plausible, but there is virtually no evidence that the rate of profit has risen over time (see Kliman 2012, especially chapters 5 and 6). Furthermore, more important than any specific pattern in the fluctuation of rate of profit is the fact that it is generally lower than it was earlier in capitalist history. This, as suggested earlier, leaves firms in a more vulnerable position during the cyclic crises that occur under capitalism. Kliman, then, leans more toward Marx's original formulation.

Another point of contention is the labor theory of value. While Marx uses it to show that capitalist exploitation is a function of the profit that is drawn from value created by the workers' labor, many modern Marxists reject it. This is not to say that they do not believe that exploitation exists, just that they specify a different source. Geoff Hodgson argues, for example, that a basic inequity exists in the fact that the worker must show up on the factory floor to sell their labor power, while the capitalist can "earn" profits on a yacht in the Carribean (Hodgson 1980). Without the former punching the clock every morning, the latter could not enjoy this lifestyle. Or one can place exploitation in the context of Rawlsian justice, wherein the question is, given how the system is organized, do I care which role I am assigned (Rawls 1971)? If one class were not exploited by the other, then people would be indifferent as to whether or not they ended up being a worker or a capitalist – but clearly they are not! Capitalism must therefore be exploitative. Last, the simple fact that workers have no option but to submit to the will of those who own the means of production is sufficient to show that they are at a significant disadvantage, regardless of what theory of justice one might employ. Note that in all these instances, class mobility only changes which individuals are exploited, not the fact that capitalism is exploitative.

Students sometimes point out at this juncture that had it not been for the capitalists, the workers would not have had a job. However, this assumes that it is necessary to have a class of individuals who earn income merely from ownership for the factories to exist. Yet even in capitalist countries, many establishments are collectively owned: public schools, libraries, fire departments, and so on. And while no one owns the University of California at Berkeley, the National Aeronautics and Space Administration, or the United States Marine Corps, all are highly respected institutions. Indeed, this would be a distinguishing feature of the immediate post-capitalist world. The capitalist class is (or will become) unnecessary.

METHOD

Because of the wide variety of applications of Marxism that exist, ranging as they do from such diverse fields as art, anthropology, and biology, it is somewhat challenging to speak of a single Marxist method. That said, one of its notable features is its consistency with Hegelian philosophy in general. For example, Marx believed it was important to distinguish between more general laws of behavior and those specific to the stage of history in question. Just because something happens under capitalism does not make it "natural," an error he thought bourgeois economists like the Classicals made with regularity. In addition, Marx insisted that we should move from abstract to concrete in theorization and not the other way around (recall Figure 4.1). In practice, this means that one cannot properly understand the economy by starting at the stage of specific, large-scale phenomena and from these derive general principles. Rather, one starts by specifying abstract general principles and then from these build the concrete whole. Trying to do otherwise can mask the true relationships under the jargon created by the relations of production specific to the current stage of history. "For example, to the capitalist and like-minded economists, wages and profit, instead of being conditioned by value, would determine value" (Fayazmanesh and O'Hara 1999, p. 705). From Marx's perspective, wages and profits cannot possibly determine value since it exists independent of them; a superficial study of capitalism, however, might lead one to think otherwise.

VIEWS OF HUMAN NATURE AND JUSTICE

As is obvious from the discussion above, the Marxist views of human nature and justice are critical components of their core theory. First, while they view humans as social animals, the key consideration in this context is class. It defines who they are and how they interact with their environment and with others. Class will also be an important determinant of their philosophical, political, religious, economic, and sociological views and the current stage of history will define what classes exist. With respect to justice, recall from the above that in a narrow sense it is specific to the stage of history in question. Profits, for example, are indeed the rightful property of capitalists under capitalism. In a broader sense, however, Marxists believe that individuals should be free to determine their fate. Under capitalism, workers are exploited and alienated. They are de facto slaves to the owners of the means of production, they are not rewarded for the whole of their economic contribution to society, and they are forced into dysfunctional relationships with themselves, their co-workers, and the product of their labor. Only under communism will human beings be free to develop their talents and pursue their dreams to the fullest extent.

STANDARDS

Primary

Because such disparate groups of people claim to be Marxists, identifying primary standards of behavior can be a little tricky. To make this more manageable, I will restrict consideration to academic economists whose work is clearly based on Marx's scholarly writings. Given that, it is probably safe to say that one is not really practicing Marxist economics if class conflict, capitalist exploitation, the existence of contradictions, or crisis are denied. These form the key framework within which economics is understood and they serve to organize and guide Marxists' analyses of capitalism. By this definition, if someone were to draw selectively from this set and take only the theory of crisis, for example, she is not a Marxist, per se. In fact, one can find each of the above concepts in one form or another in other schools of thought. Marxism is a particular specification and employment of those ideas.

Secondary

That said, one is not bound to accept all the tenets. As suggested above, there are, for example, a number of means by which one can explain exploitation. And one can still be considered a Marxist even while denying that the rate of profit declines over the long run. Baran and Sweezy still thought that internal contradictions existed that would eventually destroy the system, they just posited different ones. Maoists are still Marxists even though they see the core conflict as between urban and rural rather than capitalist and worker. None of these deny the core themes of dialectic, class, crisis, and exploitation, they only offer different characterizations thereof. As always with secondary standards, one still faces more of a battle to earn acceptance, but it can be done.

A popular research topic today is linking the Financial Crisis to the internal contradictions that will destroy capitalism. Such a connection is not difficult to see and papers making this argument can do so using either Marx's original conception, wherein speculation and fraud cause overinvestment, or with Baran and Sweezy's modifications. The same is true of the increasing maldistribution of income witnessed throughout the world. That the rich are getting richer and the poor poorer is hardly surprising to Marxists and focusing on this issue might increase one's chances of publication.

An item worthy of note in this category is that while Marxists see other non-mainstream schools of thought as allies in terms of their opposition to the existing power structure in the economics discipline, they can nevertheless be critical of what they view as naive perspectives on capitalism. For example, while the Post Keynesian approach (to be covered later in the book) agrees that capitalism is inherently unstable, they do not argue that workers are alienated or that capitalism is fraught with internal contradictions. In fact, Post Keynesian research is usually oriented toward finding means of fixing capitalism, not replacing it. Thus, while Marxists and Post Keynesians are generally friendly and have some shared views of the operation of the capitalist system, at the end of the day many Marxists would see Post Keynesians as having an unrealistic vision of the prospects for free market economies.

What this means in terms of secondary standards is that while, strictly speaking, it would be logical for Marxists to be at least moderately intellectually antagonistic toward Post Keynesians, in practice that is usually not the case. In fact, one sometimes sees Post Keynesian research in Marxist journals, Marxist research in Post Keynesian journals, and papers co-authored by scholars from each tradition. At the same time, there are, indeed, Marxist papers that attack Post Keynesian (or other) positions as bourgeois (that is, contaminated by middle-class, pro-capitalist biases).

CONTEMPORARY ACTIVITIES

Because of the wide variety of applications of Marx's work, from economics to art, there are many related conferences, associations, newsletters, working groups, and journals throughout the world. A quick Google search will reveal far more than can be reasonably covered here. But, limiting our attention to academic scholarship, *Science and Society* lays claim to being the longest-running Marxist journal, dating back to 1936. They accept a broad range of submissions and avoid limiting discussion to any particular subgroup of Marxism. *Capital and Class* and *Rethinking Marxism* are focused much more closely on economics and have been active since 1977 and 1988. The *Review of Radical Political Economics* is not an exclusively Marxist journal as it accepts work from a variety of heterodox approaches. It merits special mention because it is the official outlet for the Union for Radical Political Economics, one of the few non-mainstream groups to be allowed a presence at the American Economics Association conference. While its allotted space has been reduced over the years, it means that some Marxist research can still be presented at the major meeting of North American Neoclassical economists. This is noteworthy.

CRITICISMS

As mentioned at the beginning of this chapter, opinions about Marxism tend to be very strongly held. One common criticism focuses on Marxists' allegation that workers are de facto slaves of the capitalists and are thereby exploited and alienated. Neoclassicals and Austrians see the relationship between worker and employer as obviously mutually beneficial or the former would not choose to be associated with the latter.

Plus, is it not true that we have already tried Marxism in different countries all over the world and it failed? Not only was the Soviet Union the first communist state, but its revolution was led by a major contributor to Marxist theory in Vladimir Lenin. If it did not work there, why should we expect it to do so elsewhere? Indeed, the collapse of communism in the Soviet Union and Eastern Europe served as powerful empirical and historical evidence that Marx was wrong. The simultaneous and rapid spread of capitalism across the globe only underlines this point. Adam Smith won and Karl Marx lost and that is the end of the story.

FINAL REJOINDER

Marxists would ask first, how is it a choice when one class of people control the means of production and the other must gain access to it to live? An individual may have a limited number of options in terms of selecting one employer over another, but that is tantamount to a slave being permitted to pick one plantation over another. The choice is illusory. The reality is dependence.

With respect to the collapse of communism, what was adopted in the Soviet Union and its satellites was hardly what Marx had in mind. He was rooted more in the Western liberal tradition, where democracy and individual rights were considered foundational elements. Instead, what happened under Stalin, et al., was distinctly Russian. It drew its inspiration from their national tradition, which was much more autocratic and was only "Marxist in the sense that it was engineered by revolutionaries who considered themselves to be Marxists" (Black 1957, p. 411). After all, 1917 Russia hardly fit Marx's conception of where the revolution would start. It was supposed to occur in a capitalist country, where the exploitation of workers had created forces that led to revolution. Instead, it was in an agrarian nation ruled by a tsar, something more akin to feudalism. There has yet to be a truly Marxist revolution.

Meanwhile, what we have witnessed is precisely what Marx and Lenin predicted: the spread of capitalism all over the planet and into an increasing number of areas of our daily lives. As a consequence of capitalists' search for surplus value, today farmers farm not for subsistence, but for market; artists paint not for self-expression, but for profit; schools exist not to educate, but to generate income; and so on. And no nation will escape this. The revolution will not come until capitalism "wins." Economic disasters like the Financial Crisis will occur with increasing frequency and severity until the existing system collapses. All this is much more consistent with what we observe today than what happened in 1917 Russia.

FURTHER READING

Those wishing to know more about Marxism have quite a few options. There are, for example, a number of web pages that not only offer suggestions for further reading but host copies of key writings. The Marxist Internet Archive (http://www.marxists.org) has biographies, historical content, an encyclopedia, and access to online copies of an extremely large volume of books, articles, and letters from Marx and many others. It serves essentially as a public service. If this is a bit too heavy, In Defense of Marxism (http://www.marxist.com) has more popular writing, including interpretations of current events and audio and video resources. It also has a very useful list of basic readings, many of which are linked (search the site for "The Fundamentals of Marxism: A Short Reading List"). The World Socialist website (http://www.wsws.org) is similar and both are organs of political parties. Meanwhile, for those looking for something more advanced, there is the Union for Radical Political Economics (http://www.urpe.org) site. Last, Kapitalism 101 is an excellent source of educational materials and background (http://kapitalism101.wordpress.com/).

NOTES

1. This is a bit like saying that the sequence of inventions leading to the space shuttle must proceed as follows: glider, propeller-powered biplane, propeller-powered monoplane, jet, rocket, space shuttle. We could never arrive at the last step without first working through and resolving issues involving the earlier ones. And Marx is also arguing that the process is inevitable.
2. Much as we see today with the global spread of capitalism, including into erstwhile communist China.

REFERENCES

Baran, P.A. and P.M. Sweezy (1966), *Monopoly Capital: An Essay on the American Economic and Social Order*, New York: Monthly Review Press.

Black, C.E. (1957), "Marxism, Leninism, and Soviet communism," *World Politics*, **9** (3), 401–12.

Fayazmanesh, S. and P.A. O'Hara (1999), "Marx's methodology of political economy," in P.A. O'Hara (ed.), *Encyclopedia of Political Economy: Volume 2*, London: Routledge, pp. 704–7.

Hodgson, G. (1980), "A theory of exploitation without the labor theory of value," *Science and Society*, **44** (3), 257–73.

Kliman, A. (2012), *The Failure of Capitalist Production: Underlying Causes of the Great Recession*, London: Pluto Press.

Lenin, V.I. (1917), *Imperialism, the Latest Stage of Capitalism*, Petrograd: Parus Publishers, reprinted in 1999, Sydney: Resistance Books.

Marx, K. (1867), *Capital: Volume One*, Hamburg: Otto Meissner, reprinted in 1977, New York: Vintage Books.

Marx, K. (1885), *Capital: Volume Two*, Hamburg: Otto Meissner, reprinted in 1977, New York: Vintage Books.

Marx, K. (1894), *Capital: Volume Three*, Hamburg: Otto Meissner, reprinted in 1977, New York: Vintage Books.

Marx, K. (1959), "Critique of the Gotha Program," in L.S. Feuer (ed.), *Marx & Engels: Basic Writings on Politics and Philosophy*, Garden City, NY: Anchor Books, pp. 112–32.

Rawls, J. (1971), *A Theory of Justice*, Cambridge, MA: Belknap Press of Harvard University Press.

5. Austrian economics

The founder of Austrian economics was Carl Menger (1840–1921). In 1871, he published his *Principles of Economics*, in which he developed a unique approach to economic theorizing. His goal was not to establish a new paradigm, but to shift the focus of the mainstream and German Historical schools of economics. He actually dedicated the book to one of the leading figures in the latter, Wilhem Roscher (1817–1894), in the hope that this might make them more sympathetic. Much to his disappointment, however, his volume was either ignored or, when it was not, it was roundly criticized – especially by the very members of the German Historical school he hoped to sway (who took to calling his brand of economics "Austrian" as a pejorative). He did, however, gain a small group of followers, most notably Eugen von Böhm-Bawerk (1851–1914) and Friedrich von Wieser (1851–1926) and later Friedrich A. Hayek (1899–1992) and Ludwig von Mises (1881–1973). They were very much taken by his logic and, though not always in complete agreement, worked diligently to extend Menger's work.

Actually, for some time (roughly up to the Great Depression), Austrians were able to actively participate in mainstream economic discussions.[1] Recall, for example, that Menger was listed in Chapter 3 as one of the members of the Marginalists who were responsible for creating many of the core concepts in Neoclassical economics. Throughout, however, their work was distinct in a number of important ways. As Peter Boettke writes:

> (1) it was not mathematical, (2) it was often philosophical, (3) the dynamic nature of economic activity took center stage, and (4) it dealt with social and political issues beyond market exchange and production. (Boettke 1994, p. 2)

As the environment became less open, some Austrians suppressed these differences and moved into Neoclassicism; others continued to follow a path that led them further and further from the mainstream.

METHODOLOGICAL INDIVIDUALISM, PRAXEOLOGY, AND SUBJECTIVISM

One of the most unique aspects of Austrianism is its heavy emphasis on method. They believe that a careful analysis of the nature of the world and our ability to understand it is a logical, indeed indispensable, first step in the study of the economy. To do otherwise is the equivalent of giving a novice scientist a complex piece of equipment with no training regarding its operation or background on the character of the object to be studied. Particularly because this is an area that is almost entirely neglected in standard economics training, Austrians feel obliged to spend a considerable amount of time on this issue.

In terms of their method, the starting point is a tight focus on the individual. In the Austrian view, societies do not consume, create, invest, explore, implement social reforms, hold values, generate ideas, and so on; only individuals engage in such actions. Studies must be designed accordingly. It is also for this reason that Austrians question the use of the aggregative statistical measures so common in Neoclassicism and other schools of thought. Concepts like gross domestic product (GDP), unemployment, capital stock, and the like are viewed as historical data as they are not relevant to decision making and the actions of the decision-making individual. Econometrics and mathematical models assume quantitatively constant relationships among variables. Believing that there are no such constants in human decision making or actions because of individual free will, most Austrians prefer verbal theoretical construction.

So how do they study the economy if not by systems of equations or statistical analyses? Their guiding principle is praxeology. This method, to be explained below, is viewed by most members of the school to be their core analytical process and perhaps the key distinguishing feature of their approach – albeit not without variation and controversy (Caldwell 1984). For simplicity, I will first describe the strict version embraced by those who most closely follow Mises. There are a number of related and component concepts, starting with the action-axiom, or the proposition that every conscious action is intended to improve a person's satisfaction. This is viewed as self-evident, for the very act of trying to deny it results in evidence to the contrary: if you are trying to disprove it, then you are engaging in a conscious act aimed at achieving a desired end. Note the similarity to René Descartes's, "I think, therefore I am." To him, this too was impossible to refute, as trying to do so is evidence of thought and therefore of your own existence. The parallels do not end there. Though it would be wrong to characterize Austrians as Cartesians, it was nevertheless the goal of both Descartes and the strict praxeologists to create an impregnable argument, one composed of unquestionable premises that lead via impeccable logic to an indisputable truth. This bears repeating: to some Austrians, praxeology creates not simply a means of developing theories or discovering regularities, but of revealing the truth.

To put this in perspective, recall the sample argument from Chapter 3:

Premise 1: All economists are risk-averse.
Premise 2: Susan is an economist.
Conclusion: Susan is risk-averse.

Further recall that the above is valid if the premises support the conclusion and it is cogent if it is valid and the premises are warranted. Validity can be determined by relatively objective processes, but deciding "warranted" (and therefore cogent) is far more complex. The strict praxeologists are out to resolve this problem. They do not want warranted or close enough, they want absolutely, unquestionably correct. And they think it is possible to achieve this. This is so because the focus of our analysis is the individual, and we, ourselves, are individuals. Hence, we have a unique insight into the object of our study. Imagine the difficulties of the marine biologist or particle physicist – what they are trying to understand is completely external and foreign to them. As economists, however, we are both the analyst and the analysed. For that reason, these particular Austrians believe that introspection and reason are reliable means of developing not just reasonable, but foolproof axioms. They are very skeptical of relying on observation and falsification for the creation of assumptions. To them, there is only one proper approach and that is praxeology – the study of human action via deductive logic, based on axiomatic truths derived from self-reflection. Observation only reveals historical relationships.

This strict version is hardly universally accepted among Austrians. In fact, it is probably safe to say that is a minority view. Most either employ a diluted version thereof and/or outright reject it. Still, it is a key aspect of their method and every Austrian must at least consider her position with respect to it. There is no question, however, that it has influenced their thinking.

A more widely accepted aspect of their method is subjectivism. Austrians believe that the essence of economic behavior is personal and therefore unobservable. It is subjective, existing only in the mind of the agent. As George Selgin writes:

within the realm of human action, there are phenomena – in particular, market phenomena – that exist only by virtue of the consciousness of purposeful individuals. Thus, value, wealth, profit, loss, and cost are products of human thought, having no "objective" or extensive foundation. One cannot imagine their existence or conceive their alteration, except in connection with acts of valuation and choice. (Selgin 1988, p. 22)

Note the consistency with their focus on the individual and how it defines the categories of economic behavior upon which economists should focus. It is also another reason for their reluctance to use aggregative variables like consumer goods or capital stock. We can no more pretend that GDP is a reflection of the level of human satisfaction than we can develop a means of summing the love in a community. It is unobservable and exists only in the minds and hearts of individual agents. But it does exist.

Hence, whether or not something is a consumer good, for example, is impossible to determine a priori. This creates a problem for the identification of capital goods too, as their value is derived from the consumer goods they create. What is "capital" depends on the purpose(s) of the individual using it to some end. Much of what Neoclassical economics purports to explain in choice theory, for example, is rejected by Austrians on the basis that it assumes in evidence information that we cannot logically obtain. Subjectivism is thus key in their argument that government planning cannot be superior to market solutions. This is so because it is impossible for policy makers to know the true preferences of those they purportedly serve. Not only that, but an economy planned by government policy makers necessarily precludes private ownership of resources, and thus markets for resource exchanges. If there are no resource markets, there are no resource prices that reflect relative scarcities. Production combinations become ad hoc and arbitrary, rather than economic. This lack of information is critical and decisive and means that socialist economic reforms are bound to lead to inefficiency and stagnation – or worse. Meanwhile, in a market system, individuals are free to act based on what they and only they know and to engage in free negotiation with others who are in the same situation. No other economic system is capable of so neatly drawing out this unobservable but critical information and then using it to allocate resources and distribute goods and services. In other words, no other economic system is capable of truly satisfying our wants and needs.

MARKET PROCESS

The main focus of Austrian theory is on catallactics, or the theory of exchange. Austrians view market relations as a "real time" process involving interacting, decision-making individuals. Although the uncertainty of the future makes all decision making speculative in nature, the key thrust of Austrian market theory is to show how markets engender cooperation among exchanging individuals so that their actions are better coordinated and their individual goals thus better achieved. They do not do this consciously. Rather, such order arises spontaneously. In this manner, their methodological focus on the individual still allows for the existence of social institutions.

Austrians do not mean to imply that markets are perfect. Indeed, consumers and entrepreneurs exist in a world that is fraught with danger and about which they realistically know very little (a concept that John Maynard Keynes and the Post Keynesians also embrace – see the next chapter). So, they stumble through life, groping for answers and looking for signs that they are on the right path. They need knowledge precisely because they lack it (in stark contrast with the typical Neoclassical assumption of full information). Markets create knowledge via the prices that result from supply and demand driven by the free interaction of individuals who know, if not exactly then much better than anyone else, their own values, preferences, and so on. Markets are not perfect, but they are best. And to strict followers of praxeology, this is not theory, it is an inescapable truth.

One may wonder, incidentally, how the strict praxeologists reconcile the fact that they believe that they can identify axioms of human behavior when they also argue that only individuals know the basis upon which they act? What gives them a special power that they say no one else – particularly government policy makers – have? While this has been the subject of some controversy within Austrianism, there is a difference between claiming to know the specifics of anyone's preferences versus saying that they exist and are extremely personal. Strict praxeologists are claiming knowledge only of the general nature of economic behavior and not of information to which they could not possibly be privy.

As previously mentioned, a key to the Austrian approach is their characterization of the market as process rather than equilibrium (something they again share with Post Keynesians of the next chapter). There is no guarantee that a world in which agents are groping for the paths that will best satisfy their wants will ever reach a stable position. Indeed, the role of the entrepreneur is specifically to anticipate future consumer demand (Bostaph 2013). If entrepreneurial activity is a core feature of capitalism, then so must be change and not equilibrium.

AUSTRIAN BUSINESS CYCLE THEORY

A concrete example of the Austrian approach is their business cycle theory. Supporters describe it as:

> an altogether different kind of theory. Derived using the method Ludwig von Mises dubbed praxeology, it is the logical consequence of the axiom of human action in conjunction with its corollaries of time preference, interest, the vertical structure of production and capital complementarity, and the nature of the institution of central banking. Praxeology dispenses with mathematical tools, restricts aggregation to within individual stages of production and refrains from proffering predictions of either timing or magnitude. (Batemarco 1994, p. 216)

Consider, first, the idea that individuals will generally prefer consumption today to consumption tomorrow. To induce them to accept the latter, some reward must be offered. This is why banks must pay interest to attract savings, funds that they then loan out to firms (assuming households to be net savers and firms net borrowers). Note further that the greater their preference for today, the higher the interest rate must be to induce them to save. Now consider the resources available to the community at any given point in time. They can be employed to produce either consumer goods (what Austrians call lower-order goods) or physical capital (higher-order goods). One of the determining factors of the split between these two is the rate of interest at which firms must borrow to finance investment. If it is high, then entrepreneurs will choose to produce fewer capital goods and more consumption goods (and vice versa). This matches precisely individuals' preferences: when they want consumption today, interest rates rise and resources are diverted to consumer goods; when they are willing to wait, interest rates fall and investment rises. The market thus translates unobservable human preferences into a signal that causes agents' desires to create the preferred outcome – the specifics of which even they did not know given their limited information at the outset. No government could do this more efficiently.

Now consider what happens if the central bank decides to interfere with the market by undertaking a monetary stimulus via an extension of credit. This will have the effect of lowering interest rates and thereby encouraging a reallocation of resources from consumer goods production to capital goods production (something that adherents argue does not require a full employment assumption, only scarcity; Batemarco 1994, p. 220). Unfortunately, this is an artificial change and does not reflect individuals' preferences. This will have consequences later.

Eventually, the jump in economic activity created by the rise in investment will begin to raise prices (alternatively, one can argue that the inflation was caused by the fact that the central bank's stimulative policy required the printing of more money). This prompts officials to discontinue their earlier policy and allow interest rates to rise. Consumption will therefore rise and investment fall, and the producers of lower-order goods will find themselves unable to "bid labor, raw materials and non-specific capital goods away from the higher order capital goods industries" (Batemarco 1994, p. 217). As this occurs, some of those investments become unprofitable. Since capital goods are, as Austrians observe, not homogeneous but designed for very specific purposes, they cannot be magically transformed into factories that would be profitable in the new economic environment. Many will fail, causing economic contraction and unemployment. The underlying reason is that the expansionary monetary policy led entrepreneurs into investments that did not truly reflect consumer preferences. The resulting overinvestment caused recession and unemployment. This is precisely what they believe led to the Financial Crisis in 2007. The easy-money policies of the Federal Reserve prior to that point encouraged unproductive investments (Tempelman 2010).

Note again how this explanation focuses on the role of the individual and highlights the fact that the market is the most reliable means of translating their preferences into economic outcomes. Government attempts to stimulate the macroeconomy only served to confuse the signals sent to entrepreneurs and it led to a waste of resources.

METHOD

Because the nature of Austrianism is such that method is a key element of the school of thought, this has already been discussed at length. By way of a short summary, they adopt a strictly individualistic view of the economy in the sense that the only logical focal point is individual decision making. Aggregative concepts are not useful in theorizing, not only because of this but also since the essence of economic behavior is personal and unobservable. Strict praxeologists argue that the Austrian economics must be characterized by arguments built on a priori, axiomatic premises that then lead not to theories, but the truth. Some follow a less extreme version of this, arguing that theory requires a combination of logic and concepts taken from observation, such as, for example, the particular form of money created by central banks, which is called 'fiduciary media' and is a concept that is used in the Austrian business cycle theory. Still others believe that econometrics and formal mathematical modeling are perfectly acceptable tools of theorizing.

VIEWS OF HUMAN NATURE AND JUSTICE

As with method, their view of human nature was an integral part of the explanation above. Austrians see social behavior as ultimately the behavior of individuals. Societies do not hold values, have preferences, or make choices; individuals do. Furthermore, what drives those values, preferences, and choices is personal, subjective, and unobservable. Humans are not coldly calculating machines, carefully analysing complete sets of information. They struggle to determine the course of action that will best serve them and their lack of relevant data acts as a real hindrance, but one that can be alleviated by the signals created by markets.

Justice, to Austrians, is represented by outcomes that reflect the collective preferences of humans. And because of the subjective nature of those preferences, justice cannot be delivered by a central authority because it does not have access to the necessary information. Only markets can take these preferences and translate them into outcomes derived from what people really want. Markets are not perfect, but they are better than any other available tool for helping individuals achieve their personal goals.

STANDARDS

Primary

An absolute cornerstone is the focus on the individual interacting in market exchange. A study assuming that economic behavior is largely social in nature would not be Austrian. Likewise with respect to the subjective nature of preferences. And because of the manner in which these are incorporated into their overall approach to market theory, it is unlikely that one could manage a successful career as an Austrian while arguing that market outcomes are inferior to those generated by centralized systems. The idea that economic activity must be studied at the margin is also central, as is the concept that agents' time preferences drive both interest rates and the allocation of resources between lower- and higher-order goods.

Secondary

One need not, however, embrace praxeology in its strict form or even at all to be considered an Austrian. In fact, there is a bit of a split within the school of thought between those who more closely follow Mises and view Austrianism as a very distinct approach and the ones who are essentially Neoclassicals with a different focus (recall that it was mentioned above that some Austrians essentially joined the mainstream when the latter began to become less open to heterodox perspectives). Common themes in Austrian literature are the philosophical foundations of economic analysis, business cycles, entrepreneurship, and the role of markets in creating and using knowledge. Addressing one of these in your research is not a requirement, but could enhance your chances of publication.

Something that distinguishes Austrianism from other non-mainstream approaches is the lack of any close relationship with other heterodox schools of thought. This means that it is rare to see Austrian scholarship published in, for example, Post Keynesian or Marxist journals. Work aimed at pointing out commonalities or generating goodwill is not common and, as will be explained below, the feeling is mutual. Thus, while one might be successful in publishing a paper on the overlap between Institutionalist and Austrian economics, it would be a hard sell. Also playing a role is the fact that Austrians can sometimes enter into discussions taking place in the economic mainstream. This ability could be jeopardized if they were to openly associate with those who have been banished (though some Austrians choose to do so anyway).

CONTEMPORARY ACTIVITIES

Because Austrian economics is associated with libertarianism, there is a relatively large number of groups that espouse it. But in terms of academic research, the primary association is the Society for the Development of Austrian Economics (http://www.sdaeonline.org/). They sponsor a number of sessions at the Southern Economics Association meetings, offer several essay prizes, and are associated with the *Review of Austrian Economics*. The last represents, along with the *Quarterly Journal of Austrian Economics* (published by the Ludwig von Mises

Institute, http://www.mises.org), the main research outlet for Austrian scholars. There are also a great many discussion pages and blogs and some are even maintained by professional economists. However, the cost of starting one of these is very low and one does not have to undergo a peer-review process to post something. This does not mean that they cannot be quite good, but one should be careful not to confuse them with actual Austrian scholarship. The latter offers a much more accurate view of this school of thought.

CRITICISMS

Because they know that they are operating from a position of weakness within the discipline, most non-mainstream schools of thought avoid attacking each other. However, as suggested above, that courtesy is not always extended to the Austrians. This is so because, first, since many Austrians are able to work from within Neoclassicism, they are seen as a potential threat. Second, Austrians generally take a very pro-market stance. This clearly clashes with the Marxists, who see capitalism as exploitative. Meanwhile, even though the Post Keynesians agree with the Austrians on several key points in modeling, they use these tools to come to the conclusion that capitalism is inherently unstable and must be supplemented by government intervention. Institutionalists generally share the Post Keynesian view and most Feminists, believing that the inferior status of women is a result of social forces, take issue with the Austrian premise that economic behavior is ultimately personal. The only exception is the New Institutionalist school, some members of which adopt aspects of Austrianism in their research.

This means that Austrians come in for more than their fair share of criticism! Most common is that aimed at their individualistic approach. Institutionalists, in particular, take a starkly different stance, arguing that humans are social animals by nature and are therefore strongly influenced by culture and tradition. Most Feminists agree.

Meanwhile, Post Keynesians argue that the most significant result of assuming uncertainty is not that we need markets to create knowledge, but that physical investment breaks down and causes extended periods of involuntary unemployment (much more on this in the next chapter). In addition, they contend that the Austrian conception of inflation (part of the business cycle theory above) is flawed on a number of levels. Not only is it impossible for a central bank in a modern financial system to cause prices to rise by "printing money," but even were such a mechanism available it would only be inflationary at full employment. The economy is almost always below that level.

Marxists, of course, disagree substantially on many different points but in general see Austrians as apologists for capitalism and as being more ideological than scientific.

FINAL REJOINDER

To start, Austrians would ask the Institutionalists and Feminists, if individuals are not the ones ultimately acting, then who is? What is society other than a collection of individuals? The Roman Catholic Church or the United States of America cannot do anything, only people within them can. To argue otherwise is nonsense.

With respect to Post Keynesian objections, Austrians would first say that they are ignoring the fact that our demand for goods and services is insatiable. Because we always want more, it is impossible for demand to fall short of our total ability to supply. Unemployment may result from short-term informational problems or shocks, but such disequilibria create profit opportunities that entrepreneurs exploit, thereby rejuvenating the economy. So far as money creation leading to inflation, this is obviously true and has been shown time after time in countries like Weimar Germany and Zimbabwe. The depiction of the money supply exceeding money demand is not necessarily meant to be taken literally and is only a means of summarizing the effect of an easy money policy. Therefore, even allowing for the existence of a modern financial system, the argument still holds.

Last, to Marxists, Austrians say that the collapse of communism and the spread of capitalism – even to the People's Republic of China – speak for themselves. The fact that communist regimes have been linked to numerous human rights violations and other violent oppressive acts only furthers the case that markets are more likely to create freedom and justice than socialism.

FURTHER READING

It is probably safe to say that the Austrians, along with the Marxists, maintain the largest internet presence of any heterodox schools of thought. The Ludwig von Mises Institute (http://www.mises.org) has analyses of current events, a huge archive of literature, extensive listings of online courses, and various audio and video resources. The Austrian Economics Center (http://www.austriancenter.com) is less extensive but is especially active in sponsoring workshops and tours in Europe. The Library of Economics and Liberty (http://www.econlib.org), supported by the Liberty Fund (http://www.libertyfund.org), while not explicitly Austrian, contains a great deal that is sympathetic and offers a reading list at http://www.econlib.org/library/Topics/austrian.html.

NOTE

1. Although economics was generally more open in those days (see Malcolm Rutherford book).

REFERENCES

Batemarco, R.J. (1994), "Austrian business cycle theory," in P.J. Boettke (ed.), *The Elgar Companion to Austrian Economics*, Aldershot, UK and Brookfield, VT, USA: Edward Elgar, pp. 216–23.

Boettke, P.J. (ed.) (1994), *The Elgar Companion to Austrian Economics*, Aldershot, UK and Brookfield, VT, USA: Edward Elgar.

Bostaph, S. (2013), "Driving the market process: 'alertness' versus innovation and 'creative destruction,'" *Quarterly Journal of Austrian Economics*, **16** (4), 421–58.

Caldwell, B. (1984), "Praxeology and its critics: an appraisal," *History of Political Economy*, **16** (3), 363–79.

Selgin, G.A. (1988), "Praxeology and understanding: an analysis of the controversy in Austrian economics," *The Review of Austrian Economics*, **2** (1), 19–58.

Tempelman, J.H. (2010), "Austrian business cycle theory and the global financial crisis: confessions of a mainstream economist," *Quarterly Journal of Austrian Economics*, **13** (1), 3–15.

6. Post Keynesian economics

Although its name seems to suggest otherwise, this school of thought is about the economics of John Maynard Keynes (1883–1946). Simply "Keynesian" would have made more sense, but that moniker had already been taken – and by a group whose work the Post Keynesians claim is not very Keynes-like! In particular, the Post Keynesians argue that:

1. Those calling themselves "Keynesians" (who are, strictly speaking, members of the Neoclassical school of thought explained in Chapter 3) seriously misunderstood Keynes's central message.
2. As a consequence, while they did adopt some superficial aspects of his analysis, what they omitted were the most powerful and illuminating parts of the argument.

By contrast, Post Keynesians take as their starting point the core theory put forward by Keynes in his *General Theory of Employment, Interest and Money* (1936) and *A Treatise on Money* (1930). They have since tweaked, amended, and extended his work into areas Keynes himself had not explored.

THE GREAT DEPRESSION AND KEYNES'S GENERAL THEORY

One of the cornerstones of Post Keynesian economics is the insistence that theory and models be directly applicable to real-world problems. It is therefore not surprising that the origins of the school are closely related to a specific historical event: the Great Depression. This massive collapse in the level of economic activity, taking place as it did well before the development of widespread social safety nets, not only led to untold suffering, but created an atmosphere in which extremist politics thrived. Though the harsh conditions created by the Treaty of Versailles also helped his cause, there is little question that Adolf Hitler was able to grab and consolidate power because of the desperation of the German citizens who were affected by the slump. This connection was not lost on Keynes, who actually predicted that forcing the reparations on the Germans could lead to another war (Keynes 1920).

Economists of every variety were obviously aware of the fact that a catastrophic collapse had occurred. To Marxists, it came as no surprise. They are of the opinion that capitalism creates crises of increasing severity and in much the same manner as witnessed in the 1930s. Meanwhile, mainstream economists (not yet called Neoclassical, although sharing the same core beliefs) preached caution. In their opinion, the economy would eventually right itself and government intervention could only complicate the situation.[1] As shown in Chapter 3, they believe that the economy automatically seeks full employment equilibrium. And, to be fair, there had been other depressions (which is why this one required the adjective "Great" to differentiate it). They had, indeed, gone away after a year or two.

The Great Depression dragged on, however, one of the consequences being that erstwhile mainstream economist John Maynard Keynes came increasingly to doubt the theory he had learned. He eventually developed an alternative but this was, by his own admission, a very difficult process. As he wrote in the *General Theory*:

> The composition of this book has been for the author a long struggle of escape, and so must the reading of it be for most readers if the author's assault upon them is to be successful, – a struggle of escape from habitual modes of thought and expression. The ideas which are here expressed so laboriously are extremely simple and should be obvious. The difficulty lies, not in the new ideas, but in escaping from the old ones, which ramify, for those brought up as most of us have been, into every corner of our minds. (Keynes 1936, p. viii)

Note Keynes's implication is that it could have been a much shorter and straightforward book had it not been necessary to spend so much time explaining to the reader why the old theory was flawed. To him, that was a bigger challenge than offering his alternative – and one in which he must have largely failed or the very un-Keynes-like Keynesians would not exist. It is also important to note that Keynes saw his theory as a general one (hence the title of his book) and not applying simply to depressions or recessions. His is meant to be a theory of the economy, not of the economy under special circumstances.

UNCERTAINTY, ANIMAL SPIRITS, AND DEMAND

It is often argued that the key distinguishing feature of Keynes's model is that it assumes that economic agents operate in an environment of "uncertainty." What this means and how it affects the subsequent analysis can be difficult to grasp. To make the explanation easier, I will start with the big picture and then add detail until the specific role played by uncertainty becomes clear.

Imagine a simple economy in which we have ten workers: Alex, Bob, Charlie, Diane, Edna, Fred, Gina, Hal, Inez, and Johan. We also have one entrepreneur, Meg, and her factory is the only source of employment and income and it produces all the output in the macroeconomy. She is only willing to hire a worker if she believes she can sell the output they produce. Further, say that the productivity of Meg's factory is such that she can meet all the demands of everyone in the macroeconomy, Alex through Johan (for simplicity we will ignore what Meg consumes), using the labor of only seven of the willing workers, Alex through Gina. In other words, Meg's factory can produce sufficient output for Hal, Inez, and Johan, but there is no need to hire them to help with production. This has the following consequences:

1. Hal, Inez, and Johan will not have jobs. Hiring them would represent a cost for Meg, but there would be no benefit since she could not sell what they made. It would be in excess of the total quantity demanded.
2. Even though Meg can produce output for Hal, Inez, and Johan, she will not do so since they cannot afford to buy it. They do not have jobs.
3. Therefore, not only will Meg not hire Hal, Inez, and Johan but, if she is not producing to meet their demands, she does not even need to hire all seven of the remaining workers. Anyone whose labor would have been used to make goods for Hal, Inez, and Johan is redundant. For simplicity, let us say that is Gina.

We therefore have four involuntarily unemployed and presumably hungry workers (Gina through Johan), despite the fact that Meg has the technological ability to produce output sufficient to satisfy all their demands. This does not make Meg a bad person. She, too, has a family and perhaps shareholders who are depending on her to earn a profit. Rather, this tragically ironic outcome is a function of how the system is organized. This, according to Post Keynesians, is the critical flaw in a pure market economy. There exists insufficient demand to generate employment for every willing worker and we end up with poverty amidst the ability to generate plenty. This manifests itself both over the long run and in waves during the business cycle.

Post Keynesians argue that this parallels the Great Depression in the United States. The 1920s had been a boom period, so much so that it earned the nickname the Roaring Twenties. Unemployment fell to extremely low levels, particularly in the latter half of the decade. Then, in the 1930s, it suddenly shot up to almost 25 percent and it remained in double digits until the Second World War. And yet, the only change that had occurred in the stock of physical capital, productivity, and resources in the United States was that they had risen. The 1930s should have been a period of prosperity, the likes of which Americans had never before seen. It was not. No wonder lay people and economists alike were so confused and frustrated.

To understand the Post Keynesian argument and particularly the role of uncertainty, it is necessary to start backing up and specifying some of the unstated premises in this simple story. First and foremost, why was Alex through Johan's demand for the products sold by Meg's factory so limited? Had they wanted more, additional workers could have been employed, perhaps all of them. Some schools of thought argue just that. In particular, they say that our demand for goods and services is insatiable and that the scenario laid out by the Post Keynesians is unrealistic. People always want more, and this is why there is always sufficient demand to hire everyone who is willing to work. Unemployment and poverty are a choice or, at worst, a temporary condition that exists while the economy moves to a new full employment equilibrium position.

Post Keynesians fundamentally disagree. In part, they simply believe that human wants are satiable. We only want so many TVs, cars, houses, dinners at restaurants, college educations, and so on. What is true for a single class of goods, they argue, is true at the aggregate level as well (Jensen 1983, p. 83). Furthermore, not everything we demand requires market activity. Indeed, reading a book, enjoying your grandchildren, riding a bike, cleaning your garage, walking through the park, and so on may all give people satisfaction but have only a tenuous relationship with the part of society represented by Meg's factory.

Still, detractors say, why would someone who finds themselves with money left over at the end of the month not just go ahead and spend it? You may not derive as much pleasure from the seventh movie as you did from the first through sixth, but life is, after all, fleeting and pleasure today is better than pleasure tomorrow. You could at least frequent more expensive theaters or buy more popcorn. This is finally where Keynes's key concept of uncertainty starts to enter the analysis. It explains why you do not want to spend all your income and would like to hold some of it as cash.

Uncertainty to Keynes was a very specific concept. Consider the following situations:

1.	Perfect foresight: you are playing a card game in a casino wherein the goal is to select the color of the next card to be drawn. As the cards are face up, you will know how to place your wager. You always win!
2.	Risk: you are playing a card game in a casino wherein the goal is to select the color of the next card to be drawn. The cards are face down, but you know that one half of the cards are red and one half of the cards are black and that the deck has been randomized. You know you have a 50 percent chance of winning.
3.	Uncertainty: you are playing a card game in a casino wherein the goal is to select the color of the next card to be drawn. The cards are face down and you have only a vague idea of how many cards there are in the deck, what colors are represented, and whether or not they have been randomized. It is impossible to generate a mathematically objective idea of your chances of victory.

Keynes thought that these were critical distinctions. In a world character- ized by perfect foresight, firms, households, banks, and so on can select exactly the right action (barring their own stupidity) to maximize their welfare. Even under risk, one knows the future in a probabilistic sense. Decisions will not always be correct, but they can nevertheless be made in a calm, rational, and objective manner because you know all the possible outcomes and the likelihood of each. You do not need to have taken a statistics class to know, for example, that a number less than five is more likely on a fairly weighted, six-sided die than a number greater than five. Furthermore, you know those odds do not change just because you rolled a six this time or twice in a row or even three times. Your world is not without danger, but your forecasts are stable and your actions are relatively calm because the future can be reduced to precise mathematical probabilities. Keynes accused mainstream economics of committing this critical oversimplification.

The leap from risk to uncertainty, however, is a significant one. The latter leaves agents without any reliable reference point or anchor. For many activities whose consequences and objectives are very short term or relatively inconsequential, this is not particularly problematic. In eco- nomic matters, on the other hand, the stakes are often quite high and agents are operating with an indefinitely long time horizon. The issues created by uncertainty can therefore be very serious.

This leads to two important changes in behavior. First, it was argued above that people's demands are limited. They do not want to buy more, more, more. But even if they did, when the future is uncertain, one of the things that they want to "buy" is a buffer against what may happen in the future. That is, they want to save, and thus uncertainty reinforces agents' reluctance to spend all their income. This is the first demand-limiting effect of uncertainty and one of the reasons Post Keynesians believe that the macroeconomy can come to rest at less-than-full employment.

But just because one individual does not spend all her income does not preclude it from being spent by someone else. This is what was argued in the loanable funds theory of interest in Chapter 3. There, it was explained that banks profit by borrowing from households the income they do not want to spend and then loaning it to firms who do (on investment projects). Since it is in the banks' best interest to loan out every penny of any household savings (because that costs them money), they adjust interest rates until this is true. Thus, though this is not actually their goal, banks guarantee that every penny not spent by one person gets spent by another. In this manner, full employment is guaranteed even if individuals do not want to spend all their income.

However, Keynes believes that uncertainty enters the scene here once again and derails this happy scenario. The first question to ask is why banks pay interest. Under loanable funds, the assumption is that it is necessary to induce people to save. But Keynes says that people will save anyway because they are worried about the uncertain future. How much you are able to put aside is really a function of your earnings (the more you earn, the more you save), not whether the bank is paying 2 or 5 percent on certificates of deposit. What the latter affects is the form in which you hold those savings. People would prefer, Keynes argues, to keep their savings in cash because this is the asset most easily used to meet obligations. However, they are willing to forego this safety if offered interest. This is Keynes's liquidity preference theory of interest, wherein the latter determines how rather than how much you save.

While a complete explanation would require considerably more detail, suffice it to say that Keynes believed that his rejection of the loanable funds theory of interest in favor of his own liquidity preference was the last nail in the coffin of the full employment assumption. Consider the following scenario. Under loanable funds, a fall in investment leads banks to lower interest rates in order to get the now idle funds out of their vaults (as shown in the example in Chapter 3). This proves successful and demand remains at the full employment level because money that was not spent by one party is then guaranteed to be spent by another. But in Keynes, the process is very different. When investment falls, this has the effect of lowering household incomes as workers are laid off. With less income, they must reduce saving, and this continues until $S = I$ once again. Changes in the interest rate – which may actually rise as panic causes people to shift toward cash – play no direct role. So, whereas under loanable funds the process by which S and I returns to equality reinvigorates demand, in Keynes it is entirely possible that demand simply falls. Recession results and unemployment – which does not disappear during expansions, only diminishes – increases.

This is why Post Keynesians often argue that uncertainty, a seemingly trivial and highly abstract theoretical concept, has very significant and concrete consequences. It means that agents are satisfied before they spend their entire paycheck and that the financial system does not operate in a manner that causes the unspent income to be reinjected somewhere else. The private sector cannot be relied upon to generate sufficient demand to hire all willing workers so that, even in a perfectly operating, free market economy with plentiful resources and capital, there can be widespread joblessness. As these conditions do not encourage agents to increase spending – indeed, quite the opposite – the economy can stay like this indefinitely. Since the potential for this eventuality will increase as productivity rises over time, it points out an important and permanent role for the government. While Post Keynesians are sensitive to the fact that this gives the public sector considerable power, they also believe that no other realistic option exists. We should, indeed, develop means of controlling our politicians, but these should not come at the expense of employment, output, and our standard of living, especially when these costs would fall most heavily on the least powerful people in society.

INVESTMENT AND THE BUSINESS CYCLE

More insight can be gained into the Post Keynesian approach by examining another economic phenomenon, the business cycle. They believe that the succession of expansion and recession that we witness in the real world is not random or driven by external shocks, but systemic. Under capitalism, the conditions of expansion sow the seeds of recession, while recessions set the stage for expansion (albeit considerably more slowly than the former).

The key factor is physical investment, or the process of firms adding to productive capacity like new factories, restaurants, equipment, and so on. According to Post Keynesians, it is this rather than consumption that is most problematic. This is not to say that they do not see the maintenance of sufficient levels of consumption as important. They do, particularly in the context of economic expansion where they believe that households will eventually reach the saturation point as described above (particularly for consumer durables like automobiles and appliances). But these changes in expenditures are small as compared to the volatile swings that take place in investment. And it is investment that both drives the rest of the economy in the present and determines our ability to produce goods and services in the future.

Building new factories, retooling machines, adding new facilities, and so on are all expenditures that tend to be very expensive with consequences that reach well into the future. Whether or not a restaurant turns out to have been profitable will not be known for many years and the cost of being wrong is usually quite high, particularly because one cannot suddenly change a restaurant into a shoe store. As uncertainty means that one cannot generate objective forecasts, this makes the investment decision a very daunting one. In fact, under these circumstances one might wonder why anyone would undertake a project more consequential than a vendor's cart. Indeed, Keynes believed that a coldly calculating person would not. But he also thought that in addition to our rational selves, we exhibit a spontaneous optimism, or an urge to action rather than inaction, that he called "animal spirts":

> it is our innate urge to activity which makes the wheels go round, our rational selves choosing between the alternatives as best we are able, calculating where we can, but often falling back for our motive on whim or sentiment or chance. (Keynes 1936, p. 163)

Hence, the environment of uncertainty in which entrepreneurs operate must be offset by their animal spirits if investment is to take place. Meanwhile, the clear rule of thumb is when in doubt, do not invest!

Not only is this hesitancy consistent with the demand insufficiency story told above, but it contains the seeds of a business cycle theory. Say we start during a period when animal spirits are strong and able to overcome any misgivings created by uncertainty. This leads to the sequence of events shown in Figure 6.1.

Figure 6.1 Keynes-style economic upturn

The rising animal spirits encourage firms to believe that investments will be profitable and so they hire workers to undertake the construction of new capital. This creates additional income for households, who increase consumption (often focusing on durable items as the recovery gets underway). Since spending itself creates income, there is a further boost to spending such that this multiplier process causes the final jump in GDP to be significantly larger than the initial rise in physical investment.

Neoclassicals view such economic expansions as the normal state of affairs, one of the forces that is constantly pushing us toward full employment. But Keynes and the Post Keynesians see them as unsustainable. They argue that this is so for a number of reasons, but I will focus on only two. The first problem is that adding to physical capital does not take terribly long. A factory that may last many decades requires only a year or two to build, at most. At that point, construction workers and those in related industries are laid off. Unless, by coincidence, there are other jobs waiting for them, they become unemployed, their incomes fall, and GDP shrinks. Hence, just as investment projects are coming online and entrepreneurs are hoping to start reaping profits, they will find that sales are falling – not necessarily poor, but falling.

This would probably be sufficient to put an end to the expansion, but there is more. For, during the upturn, agents' animal spirits – encouraged by the increasing incomes and profits – continue to rise. Despite what one might assume would be relatively fresh memories of the last recession, they come to believe that good times are here to stay, if not forever then at least a little longer. Indeed, during the long US expansion of the 1990s, even experts were heard to declare it a "new economy" wherein downturns had been abolished. So, at the very time when profits moderate, expectations continue to rise. But, as sales data are collected and analysed, it will become obvious to managers and stockholders that they had been overly optimistic. Depending on the degree to which they had overestimated returns, economic agents may be in for a significant shock. And "When the disillusion comes, this expectation is replaced by a contrary 'error of pessimism'" (Keynes 1936, pp. 321–2). This can lead to widespread crisis and collapse.

The economy will remain in a slump until the memory of the collapse is sufficiently distant for agents' spontaneous optimism to take over once again. Also instrumental is the fact that existing physical capital will have become worn and new technologies and tastes may have emerged, making new projects more profitable. Then the cycle – driven not by external shocks but internal forces – starts all over again.

FINANCIAL MARKETS AND MONEY

No discussion of Post Keynesian economics would be complete without reference to financial markets. In a modern, industrial economy, many of the expenditures undertaken by firms, households, and governments are so large that they must be financed by debt. This is especially true of investment. As Keynes wrote, "banks hold the key position in the transition from a lower to a higher scale of activity" (Keynes 1937b, p. 668). No matter how clever your business plan is, it will never see the light of day if you cannot find a loan officer who shares your enthusiasm. Unfortunately, however, while financial markets are absolutely vital for the provision of liquidity, they are at the same time highly volatile. And therein lies another area (in addition to the instability of physical investment spending) where Post Keynesians say that capitalism proves to be prone to crisis.

Consider first the avenues by which financial markets affect the economy, particularly its key driver, investment. Among the funding choices available to firms are borrowing from banks and other financial institutions and the sale of stock. In the former case, those approving loans will be subject to the same forces as their customers. Just as entrepreneurs are affected by the interplay of uncertainty, animal spirits, hope, and disappointment described above, so are bankers. Because they will be reacting to the same phenomena at the same time, they will tend to be somewhat in sync; but if they are not, then investment spending will be constrained and this creates yet another obstacle to generating sufficient demand to reach full employment. In addition, it is not enough that the financial sector be willing to extend credit, it must also be able. For this reason, Post Keynesians argue that financial crises and credit crunches add yet another impediment.

For firms that opt to sell stock, they will, of course, only receive proceeds on the initial offer. Subsequent transactions simply transfer ownership and do not add a penny to the company's coffers. But, even then, the fluctuation of their stock price still has an impact on the firm's viability. For example, if the firm decides to undertake further issuances of stock, the current price will determine how much it can rise. Or, if the firm chooses to borrow from a bank that institution will most certainly consider the price of the firm's outstanding shares in evaluating its creditworthiness. Last, if a stock price falls too far, stockholders may move to replace the management team.[2] Firms are thus affected by financial markets in a number of ways, both direct and indirect.

Given these connections, it is important that financial markets price assets and allocate funds efficiently. In order to do this, bankers and stock market participants must generate reasonably accurate forecasts of which firms will be the most profitable so that those companies will get the largest share of loans at the best terms and have the stocks with the highest prices. It is not necessary that these be exactly correct, of course, but the process by which they are formed should at least be relatively stable and based on factors that are consistently correlated with the firms' success.

The first problem, however, is that the environment of uncertainty in which we live prevents us from making mathematically objective predictions. Post Keynesians contend that this tends to make our forecasts and consequent behavior unstable. To understand this, consider what would happen if the world were only risky (as per the definitions above). We would not know for certain which firms would outperform others, but we could nevertheless reduce the future to definitive probabilities. Say, for example, that you know that there is a 75 percent chance that firm A's monthly profits will exceed firm B's and you have created a portfolio of assets with this in mind. Now assume that after the first month it is actually firm B's profits that are higher. Do you rush to your broker to sell off all your firm A stock? Of course not. What if this happens two months in a row, something that is unlikely but nevertheless possible? You would still not panic or probably even change the composition of your portfolio because, so long as it remains true that firm A has a 75 percent chance of earning higher profits than firm B, your financial investments will have been based on objective mathematical calculations.[3] Some tweaking may occur, but no large-scale changes are likely. Behavior under risk is therefore very stable, even when people are disappointed.

This is not true under uncertainty. When we do not know all the possibilities nor their probabilities, "there is no scientific basis on which to form any calculable probability whatever. We simply do not know" (Keynes 1937a, p. 214). But, despite this fact,

> the necessity for action and for decision compels us as practical men to do our best to overlook this awkward fact and to behave exactly as we should if we had behind us a good Benthamite calculation of a series of prospective advantages and disadvantages, each multiplied by its appropriate probability, waiting to be summed. (Keynes 1937a, p. 214)

In other words, we have to behave as if we have sufficient information. However, with no solid anchor underpinning our actions, rapid and sometimes panicked changes are now possible. This is especially likely when market participants are disappointed. Depending on the degree of error, they may shift frantically between one stock and another, trying desperately to minimize losses and stabilize the value of their portfolios – something that will have the opposite effect if everyone is pursuing this strategy at once. And, if forecasts and agents' behavior are unstable, then so will be prices. This is not conducive to a smoothly operating financial system.

Not only that, but there is no set of widely recognized, basic factors upon which we can focus in making our forecasts. Financial market participants could do their best to generate such a list and there are certainly more and less useful factors. No one is going to include the color of the paint used to mark the parking spaces at the company in question, while everyone is going to be interested in last quarter's profits. But what else should be included in determining the future profitability of the asset issuer, especially given the dynamic nature of the economy and the long time horizon of such a forecast? In order to do this properly, one would need to understand the specific market in which the firm competes, their plans for future operations, any relevant government regulations (current and potential), the effectiveness of their management team, possible labor issues, factors affecting the price and availability of inputs, the determinants of the customers' demand, and so on and so on. Plus, one would need to research this for each of their competitors and for firms in other industries where one might also be considering buying stock. This is, to say the least, an extremely difficult undertaking.

Forecasting short-term market psychology, on the other hand, is much easier. It requires no in-depth knowledge of the complex and myriad issues affecting the asset issuer, only a basic understanding of human behavioral tendencies like bandwagons, profit taking, and fads. Furthermore, this knowledge is transferred easily from one asset category to another and it promises quick returns. Keynes argued that this was, in fact, what most skilled financial investors actually did, trying to "outwit the crowd" by guessing what everyone else is guessing rather than working to truly determine which firms were most likely to generate profits over the long term (Keynes 1936, p. 155).

He further argued that those choosing the latter, while doing something much more socially useful because it would make asset prices more closely related to firm viability, were making their own jobs much more difficult. "He who attempts it must surely lead much more laborious days and run greater risks than he who tries to guess better than the crowd how the crowd will behave; and, given equal intelligence, he may make more disastrous mistakes" (Keynes 1936, p. 157). Those holding for the long term must also have greater-than-average access to financial resources since they will have to weather the short-term fluctuations created by speculation. Furthermore, they may have to convince their supervisors or customers that bucking the current trend and holding for the long run is really the most rational course of action. The upshot of all this is that financial asset prices are heavily, if not exclusively, influenced by short-term psychological factors.

Thus, financial asset prices and the markets in which they are set, while terribly important for the provision of liquidity, are unstable and driven by factors often only tangentially related to the asset issuer's prospects. That said, Keynes is keen to point out that this does not mean that we witness wild volatility on a daily basis (Keynes 1936, pp. 162–3). But, even though panics, booms, and the misallocation of resources caused by mispriced stocks may not cause problems continuously, when those problems emerge they can be very serious and we should not be surprised they occurred.

Post Keynesians argue that part of this is unavoidable. Nothing can change the fact that the world is uncertain and it is thus inevitable that forecasts will always tend to be somewhat unstable. But it is perfectly within our means to force market participants' attention away from short-term psychology. Keynes half-jokingly suggests that we should accomplish this by making stock ownership permanent because "this would force the investor to direct his mind to the long-term prospects and to those only" (Keynes 1936, p. 160). Indeed, if you thought that once you bought a share of stock that you had to hold it forever, you would do a great deal of research! Analyses of market psychology would be useless and for this reason Post Keynesians believe that it would generate a more socially useful outcome. Of course, it is not necessary to go to such extremes to reach this goal. One could, for example, introduce a sliding-scale transactions tax that declined the longer one held an asset. This would not only force financial investors to think more about the long-term viability of the asset issuer, thus making prices more closely reflect this, but would dampen short-term volatility by introducing a cost to quick selling. Post Keynesians believe, incidentally, that the above characterization of the financial market offers a much better framework for understanding the Financial Crisis of 2007–08. Short-term psychological factors drove asset prices to levels that coldly rational observers would never have thought sustainable. And, once it was evident that this was true, everyone rushed for the exits.

METHOD

There is a large and growing literature that sets out to identify a clearly defined Post Keynesian method, both in terms of description (looking at how research is done now and was done in the past) and prescription (how it should be done in the future). But perhaps the best starting point is with an extended quote from Keynes himself:

The object of our analysis is, not to provide a machine, or method of blind manipulation, which will furnish an infallible answer, but to provide ourselves with an organised and orderly method of thinking out particular problems; and, after we have reached a provisional conclusion by isolating the complicating factors one by one, we then have to go back on ourselves and allow, as well as we can, for the probable interactions of the factors amongst themselves. *This is the nature of economic thinking.* Any other way of applying our formal principles of thought (without which, however, we shall be lost in the wood) will lead us into error. It is a great fault of symbolic pseudo-mathematical methods of formalising a system of economic analysis, such as we shall set down in section vi of this chapter, that they expressly assume strict independence between the factors involved and lose all their cogency and authority if this hypothesis is disallowed; whereas, in ordinary discourse, where we are not blindly manipulating but know all the time what we are doing and what the words mean, we can keep "at the back of our heads" the necessary reserves and qualifications and the adjustments which we shall have to make later on, in a way in which we cannot keep complicated partial differentials "at the back" of several pages of algebra which assume that they all vanish. (Keynes 1936, pp. 297–8, emphasis added)

He is saying a great deal that is consistent with the work of later Post Keynesian authors, but in a language that is more accessible. First off, it is evident that he thinks that the economy is too complex to be successfully reduced to a system of equations or a set of presumably law-like behaviors and relationships ("a machine, or method of blind manipulation"). The everything-else-being-equal condition never holds in the real world so that, strictly speaking, any model making that assumption may have only limited applicability. Furthermore, behaviors are rarely independent of one another – a shift of the supply curve may well set into motion forces that then shift the demand curve, raising questions about equilibrium analysis. This does not mean that we should surrender and stop theorizing and building models entirely, but we must do so in the context of a belief that all such efforts are inevitably tentative and exploratory. Post Keynesians say that economies are open systems, meaning that "one does not know all the relevant variables" (Dow 2001, p. 16).

This does not mean that attempts to explain economic behavior are futile, however. While, according to Post Keynesians, all economic theorizing by every school of thought is subject to the problems described above, the real issues arise when one ignores this fact. Post Keynesians view their analyses as more useful precisely because they acknowledge their limitations. By contrast, they view with great skepticism the claims of schools of thought who see their research as "proving" the existence of particular relationships or uncovering truths.

With the above caveats in mind, Post Keynesians place a great deal of emphasis on understanding the causal linkages in real-world processes. They do not agree with the Neoclassicals and Austrians that we should rely more on abstract reasoning than observation and they believe that the cogency of arguments is a function of the degree to which premises match what we see around us. Models based on counterfactuals or as-if assumptions are viewed with suspicion. Simplification and generalization are necessary, but, as the real world is the perfect model of itself, it is always the standard against which Post Keynesians judge their efforts. Modeling by analogy is frowned upon.

Also important to Post Keynesian method are the concepts of uncertainty, non-ergodicity, and historical time. The first was explained at length above and was shown to be the reason Post Keynesians believe people are willing to hold cash and that the economy can come to rest at less-than-full employment. Non-ergodicity says that economic behavior today may not follow the same patterns as yesterday. Hence, even if we were able to build a perfect model of the economy at this moment, that does not mean it will apply one, five, or ten years from now. Institutions evolve, cultures change, and humans adapt. Though we do not necessarily need a brand-new model every month, Post Keynesians believe that it is very important to bear in mind that economic behavior is not law-like and constant. Finally, they see the world as existing in historical rather than mechanical time. In mechanical time, the order of events is unclear and cannot be determined without additional assumptions. Take, for example, a market diagram with a single supply curve and two demand curves. Which of the latter came first and which is the result of a shift? It is impossible to know, and that is the nature of mechanical time. Either could be first and either could be second, so that time could move in either direction. Historical time, on the other hand, envisions a path-dependent world, where the past changes what is possible in the future. The Great Depression forever shifted the world economy onto a new track. The fact that you decided to go to college means that where you will find yourself in five years will be different than had you gone straight into the workforce or joined the military. When I was twenty-two I went to a party at my friend Paul's apartment; there I met and later married a girl named Melanie and we now have twin daughters. In each case, understanding the process by which one event leads to another is very important and the direction is one-way. This is not the case when comparing two equilibrium positions.

VIEWS OF HUMAN NATURE AND JUSTICE

Post Keynesians see humans as social animals, meaning that the rules of the game are more important than individual motivations in driving economic behavior. In their view, the specific structure of institutions holds the key to understanding the way the world works. Economic justice is anchored in the conviction that every citizen must have a realistic opportunity to share in the output produced in an economy. Post Keynesians believe that the level of productivity possible in modern economies is such that it is downright immoral to exclude anyone who is willing to work – and people are not lazy, they want to work.

Because of this, justice requires that the government achieve what the private sector cannot: full employment. And while they agree with some other schools of thought regarding the primacy of fiscal policy in this effort, Post Keynesians are not keen on the manner in which it is practiced today. Currently, the usual approach is for the government to spend in deficit in order to raise private sector sales and thereby hope to indirectly induce firms to offer more jobs. While not useless, Post Keynesians say this is inefficient and ultimately ineffective because it never reaches the chronically unemployed. Many would prefer to see the government directly address the problem by offering a job guarantee (Tcherneva 2012). Under such a system, those unable to secure employment in the private sector, including those with the least saleable job skills, would always have the option of working in the public sector. The latter would offer training along with an income and would be designed to supplement, not replace, the private sector.

STANDARDS

Primary

Primary standards specific to Post Keynesianism include the rejection of the full employment assumption and a related concept, the belief in fundamental uncertainty. A model premised on the idea that the economy self-corrects or automatically generates a job for every willing individual would simply not be Post Keynesian. The whole point of the adjective "general" in the title of Keynes's magnum opus was to highlight that his approach would allow for less-than-full employment equilibrium. Furthermore, this was accomplished by his assumption of the existence of uncertainty in the macroeconomy. As shown above, uncertainty enters into Post Keynesian analysis at a number of levels and is a fundamental concept. Rejecting this means you are no longer in the Post Keynesian club.

One of the other impacts of uncertainty is in the financial market, where asset prices are unlikely to be accurate reflections of the long-term profitability of the issuer. Hence, financial markets may be capable of supplying liquidity, but it is difficult for them to efficiently allocate resources. In the microeconomy, it is a basic tenet of Post Keynesianism that the emergence of oligopoly power is common and it is key in understanding pricing, the distribution of income, and inflation.

Methodologically, Post Keynesians self-consciously reject the as-if method and in contrast emphasize the placement of theory in the context of specific historical and institutional structures. Causal linkages are very important and thus a paper making the assumption that the central bank increases the money supply by dropping cash from a helicopter (as in a classic article by Neoclassical economist, Milton Friedman) would stand little chance of publication in a Post Keynesian journal.

Secondary

Like all other schools of thought, there are important authors whose citation tends to lend credibility to an argument independent of the idea being expressed. John Maynard Keynes is obviously foremost in this regard, followed by others like Paul Davidson, Alfred Eichner, James K. Galbraith, John Kenneth Galbraith, Michael Kalecki, Nicholas Kaldor, Jan Kregel, Hyman Minksy, Joan Robinson, and Sidney Weintraub. As with other secondary standards, one is free to disagree with one of these pillars of Post Keynesianism and still be considered a member of the community, but the burden of proof is on the rebellious scholar.

There are also common themes in the Post Keynesian literature, inclusion of which in a model or theory may enhance the chances of publication and the popularity of research but about which there is not complete agreement. For example, some Post Keynesian authors insist that the supply of money is completely demand driven in the sense that whenever demand rises, the financial sector is able to accommodate without it being necessary for the central bank to undertake any discretionary policy. Others agree that this is true but only to an extent. There has also been disagreement over the nature of inflation, with early Post Keynesians marking wage increases above the level of productivity as the culprit. Later practitioners saw this as unfairly and inaccurately blaming labor power. There is also some disagreement of the effect of interest rates on physical investment, with all Post Keynesians seeing it as a secondary factor but some as having no impact at all. Perhaps most interesting is the division that exists regarding what should be included under the heading "Post Keynesian." While all would agree that what has been described in this chapter belongs, there are also those who believe that the neo-Ricardian, Sraffian, or Kaleckian approaches should also be included. These focus more on the role of income distribution in the macroeconomy and, while they do not exclude the possibility of funda-mental uncertainty as a key factor in the instability of the capitalist system, they do not rely on it. Thus, something that many would argue was central to Keynes's revolution is missing. Is this "Post Keynesian" or not? Both arguments have been made.

CONTEMPORARY ACTIVITIES

The primary outlet for Post Keynesian research is the *Journal of Post Keynesian Economics*. It was founded in 1975 by leading Post Keynesian economists Sidney Weintraub and Paul Davidson. The *Cambridge Jour-nal of Economics*, *International Review of Applied Economics*, *Review of Political Economy*, *Review of Radical Political Economy* (primarily Marxist), and *Journal of Economic Issues* (primarily Institutionalist) also welcome Post Keynesian contributions. Though they do not have their own formal association, it is not uncommon to see them as members of Institutionalist economic groups like the Association for Evolutionary Economics and the Association for Institutional Thought. Post Keynes-ians not only frequently present papers at their conferences, but they even hold offices in their societies. The strong link between Post Keynesian economics and Institutionalism is an interesting one, but as the latter is the subject of the next chapter, further discussion of that phenomenon will have to wait.

One area of Post Keynesian economics that has become increasingly active and has attracted quite a bit of media attention is called Modern Monetary Theory (MMT). While it embraces everything above, its specific focus has been the role of the federal government's budget. Recall the discussion of the job guarantee. How can this be financed? Surely those countries most desperately needing it, that is, those with the highest levels of unemployment and the lowest rates of growth, are also those least able to afford it? Adopting a jobs guarantee could be terribly expensive and cause the federal government to run large budget deficits and accumulate a great deal of debt. Thus, it may be that we simply cannot afford to reduce unemployment.

Supporters of MMT argue that this is nonsense and based on a fundamental misunderstanding of how federal government budgeting operates and what really creates wealth. The latter is a function of an economy's ability to produce goods and services, not the volume of cash it has accumulated. Money is simply a computer entry and, in countries like the United States or the United Kingdom that issue their own currency and are not in a fixed exchange system, it can be created at will. It is decidedly not wealth and in such countries any monetary cost of a jobs program is therefore irrelevant. The true cost is that associated with allowing labor to remain idle and rob us of the output they would have created (and the unemployed of incomes and dignity). It is for this reason that MMT supporters say that we cannot afford not to have a job guarantee and that there is no level of debt a government with its own currency cannot repay. Ironically MMT also suggests that budget deficits would actually be smaller under a job guarantee since the money would be properly focused and the policy would generate more taxable income.

Because these views contrast so sharply with those of the many pundits and politicians predicting catastrophic US and UK (among others) government defaults, proponents of MMT have found their work in the news (see, for example, Lowrie 2013; Matthews 2012). It is noteworthy, too, that while MMT has a Post Keynesian framework, many of those active in the movement are not economists, per se.

CRITICISMS

Post Keynesianism has been accused of being more focused on attacking Neoclassical ideas than forwarding their own. It is easy to criticize others as being unrealistic when every model is by definition a simplification. Post Keynesianism is, therefore, not so much a unified school of thought than a group of disparate scholars who complain about those in the mainstream. This characterization is reinforced by the fact that neo-Ricardians, Sraffians, and Kaleckians, all groups with no direct connection to Keynes, also sometimes count themselves as Post Keynesians. What is most likely, say some, is that these economists simply do not understand the advanced mathematics used in Neoclassical economics.

Post Keynesians also receive criticism from within heterodoxy, where more left-leaning schools of thought see them as apologists for capitalism. What this means is that while they concede that the market system is by nature prone to breakdown, Post Keynesians naively believe that capitalism is really okay and we should just fix rather than replace it.

FINAL REJOINDER

Post Keynesians would argue that while it is quite true that they do, indeed, spend some time criticizing the foundations of Neoclassicism, this is necessary if they are going to explain their approach to those already educated in the mainstream. Furthermore, they clearly have distinct and well-developed methods and models and an extensive literature of their own. And it is not that Post Keynesians cannot understand the mathematical formalization typical of Neoclassicism, but that they agree with Keynes (who was an excellent mathematician):

> Too large a proportion of recent "mathematical" economics are mere concoctions, as imprecise as the initial assumptions they rest on, which allow the author to lose sight of the complexities and interdependencies of the real world in a maze of pretentious and unhelpful symbols. (Keynes 1936, p. 298)

Hence, according to Post Keynesians, the problem is not that they do not understand the mathematics necessary to make sense of the economy, but that Neoclassicals do not understand the economy well enough to know how to properly employ mathematics.

Meanwhile, with respect to being apologists for capitalism, they would respond that they are simply pragmatic. Markets are tools and they, like any other tool, work well in some contexts and not in others. They have no inherent moral aspect and are neither evil nor virtuous on their own. Injustices exist, to be sure, but there is no reason to believe that these would be remedied by a wholesale rejection of the capitalist system.

FURTHER READING

Obviously, Keynes's *General Theory* is the key volume for Post Keynesians, but it can be a difficult read even for economists (although chapters 12 and 22 are very illuminating and could be read easily). A relatively technical though much clearer exposition is Victoria Chick's *Macroeconomics After Keynes* (1983). Another classic work is Paul Davidson's *Money and the Real World* (1972); again, however, it is likely too advanced for the introductory-level student. His *The Keynes Solution* (2009) may be more appropriate, as would be Marc Lavoie's *An Introduction to Post-Keynesian Economics* (2010). Richard Holt and Steven Pressman's *A New Guide to Post Keynesian Economics* (2001) offers short introductions to specific topics authored by various Post Keynesian scholars.

Online resources include *Social Democracy for the 21st Century* (socialdemocracy21stcentury.blogspot.com), which not only has blog entries on various current issues but a comprehensive reading list (search for Post Keynesian Economics 101 on the site). *New Economic Perspectives* (neweconomicperspectives.org) focuses on MMT and is based in the economics department at the University of Missouri at Kansas City. It includes a primer on money creation and financing federal government spending. Other Post Keynesian blogs include *The Case for Concerted Action* (http://www.concertedaction.com), *Fixing the Economists* (fixingtheeconomists.wordpress.com), and *Naked Keynesianism* (nakedkeynesianism.blogspot.com). Of note, too, is the Levy Economics Institute (http://www.levyinstitute.org), a Post Keynesian research institute that publishes a large number of policy and scholarly papers, plus hosts conferences.

NOTES

1. Not that the mainstream spoke with a single voice.
2. If banks securitize any loans (which essentially means that they divide them into packets and sell them, as happened with the subprime mortgage market in the United States) then those securities can have many of the same characteristics of stocks.
3. Note that a more realistic example would also consider the impact of the different rates of profit expected and the price of each stock. But as this would only complicate the example and not change the conclusion (that is, agents' forecasts and subsequent behavior would still be very stable), I opted to keep it simple.

REFERENCES

Chick, V. (1983), *Macroeconomics After Keynes: A Reconsideration of the General Theory*, Cambridge, MA: MIT Press.

Davidson, P. (1972), *Money and the Real World*, London: Macmillan.

Davidson, P. (2009), *The Keynes Solution: The Path to Global Economic Prosperity*, New York: Palgrave Macmillan.

Dow, S.C. (2001), "Post Keynesian methodology," in R.P.F. Holt and S. Pressman (eds), *A New Guide to Post Keynesian Economics*, London: Routledge, pp. 11–20.

Holt, R. and S. Pressman (2001), *A New Guide to Post Keynesian Economics*, London: Routledge.

Jensen, H.E. (1983), "J. M. Keynes as a Marshallian," *Journal of Economic Issues*, **17** (1), 67–94.

Keynes, J.M. (1920), *The Economic Consequences of the Peace*, New York: Harcourt, Brace and Howe.

Keynes, J.M. (1930), *A Treatise on Money*, New York: Harcourt, Brace and Company.

Keynes, J.M. (1936), *The General Theory of Employment, Interest and Money*, London: Macmillan.

Keynes, J.M. (1937a), "The general theory of employment," *Quarterly Journal of Economics*, **51** (2), 209–23.

Keynes, J.M. (1937b), "The 'ex-ante' theory of the rate of interest," *Economic Journal*, **47** (188), 663–9.

Lavoie, M. (2010), *An Introduction to Post-Keynesian Economics*, Basingstoke, Hampshire: Palgrave Macmillan.

Lowrie, A. (2013), "Warren Mosler, a deficit lover with a following," *New York Times*, July 4, available at http://www.nytimes.com/2013/07/05/business/economy/warren-mosler-a-deficit-lover-with-a-following.html (accessed March 28, 2014).

Matthews, D. (2012), "Modern Monetary Theory, an unconventional take on economic strategy," *Washington Post*, February 18, available at http://www.washingtonpost.com/business/modern-monetary-theory-is-an-unconventional-take-on-economic-strategy/2012/02/15/gIQAR8uPMR_story.html (accessed March 28, 2014).

Tcherneva, P. (2012), "Permanent on-the-spot job creation – the missing Keynes plan for full employment and economic transformation," *Review of Social Economy*, **70** (1), 57–80.

7. Institutionalism

Institutionalism was once one of the dominant paradigms in the United States. It boasted several presidents of the American Economics Association and its members participated as equals in an active and lively scholarly exchange with Neoclassical economists. Early Institutionalist John R. Commons (1862–1945) and his followers were pioneers in practical applications of economic theory. They undertook extensive empirical work on the business cycle and played a major role in the establishment of the National Bureau of Economic Research, an organization that remains one of the most important think tanks in the world and is the official authority for the dating of expansions and recessions in the United States. Another early Institutionalist, Thorstein Veblen (1857–1929), wrote complex, critical analyses of American economic behavior and some of the terms he coined (conspicuous consumption, for example) became a part of our everyday language.

And yet, despite all this, today there is possibly no other school of thought that seems more foreign to the average economist than Institutionalism. Take, for example, this passage from a classic work by Paul Dale Bush:

> The institutional structure of any society incorporates two systems of value: the ceremonial and the instrumental, each of which has its own logic and method of validation. While these two value systems are inherently incompatible, they are intertwined within the institutional structure through a complex set of relationships. (Bush 1987, p. 1079)

This appears to have absolutely nothing in common with the discussions of investment, unemployment, marginal cost, equilibrium, entrepreneurs, and so on that one finds in other schools of thought in this book. Indeed, most economists would say that it fails one of the discipline's key primary standards: subject matter. It is not, they would contend, economics at all, but sociology. To Institutionalists, however, not only is this economics, but it is on a much deeper and far more significant level than that approached by other schools of thought. One cannot possibly understand modern capitalism, they contend, without laying bare the value structure that legitimizes it. It is the latter that truly drives

economic activity, not fiscal policy, the tax structure, or capital expenditures. Those are mere details.

The path to understanding their perspective must start with the concept
that *Homo sapiens* are social animals. Nothing else is more fundamental
to their view. We live, eat, reproduce, grow, and die in packs. This is as
instinctive to us as it is to wolves, chimpanzees, ants, or bees. No
individual animal in any of those species consciously chooses to live with
the others, it is hard wired into them because it evolved as a survival
mechanism. Institutionalists further argue that none of the evidence of
our prehistory indicates that we once lived by ourselves and then
decided, via social contract, to surrender some of our "freedoms" to live
together. Humans have always been social because it is as natural to us as
bipedal locomotion or live birth. This has, to Institutionalists, immense
consequences, not the least of which is that the basic building block of a
study of economic behavior must be culture, not the individual.

This emphasis on evolution and culture represented (and continues to
represent) a fundamental departure from the equilibrium analysis and
methodological individualism that dominates the mainstream. Part of the
reason for the shift was that these were brand-new and exciting concepts
in Veblen's day. Just as Adam Smith, born a few years before Isaac
Newton's death, was so influenced by the latter's ideas that he adopted
the natural-law metaphor for our science, so Veblen did the same with
Charles Darwin (1809–1882) and the work of the first modern anthropologists. But there was more to the transformation than simply the
novelty of these new approaches. The United States in the late nineteenth
century was a "world of growing industrialization and rapid socioeconomic change," giving budding Institutionalists ample subject matter
for their new approach (Mayhew 1987, p. 991). They believed that it
showed very clearly that economic structures and behavior changed over
time, just as species do, and that the operative mechanism was culture.
That all economists were not similarly inspired was because, say
Institutionalists, they had already accepted the Newtonian view so
completely that they could not see beyond it (as with the Neoclassicals)
or they already had their own theory of capitalist transformation (as with
the Marxists).

But for Institutionalists, the combination of Darwin's evolutionary
theories, the discovery of the concept of culture, and the transformation
of American capitalism pointed to a new way of understanding economies. It began with the idea that all behavior is continually evaluated as
being either appropriate or inappropriate. Those acts judged as falling
into the former win approval and status for the individual – things every
bit as important to us *Homo sapiens* as food, shelter, and clothing. The

alternative can lead to formal and informal sanctions ranging from not being invited to a party to imprisonment or execution. For the most part, however, such penalties are not necessary as we each instinctively strive to voluntarily meet the standards of our reference group. Sometimes our conformity occurs on a conscious (or, perhaps more appropriately, self-conscious) level, for example, when we are trying to gain membership of an exclusive club or when you are the new kid at school. But it is, generally speaking, subconscious and automatic because cultural conformity is in our nature. It is part of what makes us human and how we identify with our tribe – and we need a tribe to survive.

This is not to say that there are not times when people rebel against norms; instances with any significance, however, involve those people acting together.[1] Those who opposed segregation in the American South, for example, represented an entire subculture (not just a few individuals) with competing ideas of right and wrong. What each side in this deeply divisive debate viewed as appropriate behavior was mutually exclusive. Each group tried its best to bring to bear formal and informal sanctions, including acts of terror and violence, which would force the opposition to submit to their ideals and thereby change (or maintain, in the case of segregationists) the general value structure of the society. And note that in the end, while the de-segregationists were victorious, this did not mean that the segregationists simply accepted it. For the overwhelming majority of that group, their minds had not been changed and they did whatever they could to continue to encourage the behavior of which they approved. However, the scales had been tipped and as new generations of Southerners grew up, attitudes adjusted – not completely, but substantially. This is consistent with the Institutionalist belief that true cultural change takes a very long time because the values are so deeply seated during the process of acquiring them. Incidentally, segregationists and de-segregationists, having had many common social experiences, inevitably shared values too.

Note the importance of the role of power in the above. Institutionalists believe that this must be taken into account in economic analyses. Wages, for example, are decisively affected by it. While one's productivity is certainly a factor, it is not, as argued in some other schools of thought, the only one. Women, Blacks, and other such groups, Institutionalists say, would attest to this. Institutionalists also argue that it is much easier to recognize historical rather than contemporary injustices because we find it extremely difficult to critique that which is a function of values we take for granted.

This also points out the embeddedness of the economy with respect to the rest of the society. It is not separate or distinct, but a function of, intimately connected to, and consistent with the larger culture. Markets reflect and reward the values of the market participants. For example, if in the 1950s a non-racist entrepreneur in the American South decided to hire a Black woman to sell jewelry at his shop, he would very likely experience, at the very least, a fall in sales, if not outright violence. If the entrepreneur wishes to stay in business, then he is forced to replace her with a White employee, regardless of the Black woman's qualifications and regardless of his social views. Where the culture is racist, the market is racist because the market is simply one of the means by which the culture expresses its values. This has the effect of reinforcing them, for even the non-racist entrepreneur must take them into account if he is to stay in business. Note that this view is in stark contrast to arguments from schools of thought that believe the market destroys racism since it encourages color-blind employment policies guided solely by the qualifications of the applicant. This, according to Institutionalists, is more than naive; it represents a fundamental misunderstanding of economic behavior.

Is this economics or sociology? To the Institutionalist, it is difficult to imagine anything more important to the economic wellbeing of Americans in the South throughout this period than racism. It was the prime determinant of wages, incomes, employment prices, migration, industry, education, and so on. It shaped the entire landscape and entered into every part of people's lives. How can this, they ask, not be economics?

THE INSTITUTIONALIST APPROACH

Note that such an analysis requires a very different skill set than most economists learn. The Institutionalist must delve deeply into the history, structure, power relationships, politics, and so on of any society to begin to get a sense of the values that drive the economy. Simply taking account of GDP, interest rates, wages, and so on is not sufficient. Many non-Institutionalist economists view this as a-theoretical exercise in which the researcher is simply describing without a larger theoretical framework, something that they see as prone to unconstrained speculation and bias. This is decidedly untrue, say Institutionalists, and a function of the fact that outsiders just do not recognize the method that is being applied. There is, in fact, a carefully considered and long-established general theory of the economy. The key organizing concept is the idea that all values fall inevitably into one of two categories: they are either ceremonial or instrumental. And while it is a gross oversimplification to say that the former is bad and the latter good, it is a decent place to start. Economies dominated by ceremony stagnate; those driven by instrumentality develop. And yet adherence to ceremony is an integral part of being human.

✳ Ceremonial values are past-binding and oriented toward defining status and acceptable behavior in a society. Behaviors sanctioned by ceremony derive their legitimacy not from logic or experimentation, but from authority. These values are so deeply ingrained in us that it is difficult to recognize them. Indeed, we may vigorously argue that we are choosing to act this way because it is eminently logical to do so. But this is not really true. Why, in the United States, do women take their husband's last name in marriage, men wear strips of brightly colored cloth tied around their necks for formal occasions, people maintain eye contact as a sign of honesty, and so on? None of these is universal among humans and it would not have been possible to logically predict them in any scientific way. Alternative behaviors could just as easily have evolved and did so in other cultures. But we would find theirs terribly uncomfortable and even ridiculous, the very definition of "foreign." Ceremonial behaviors are thus culturally relative: they make sense only in the societies where they are practiced. They derive their legitimacy from their connection to tradition.[2]

You would think that as a consequence we would take ceremonial values with a grain of salt and exhibit considerable tolerance for deviations, but usually the opposite is true. This is because these ritualistic behaviors represent a vitally important part of our sense of belonging to the tribe. Challenging these behaviors can be very upsetting to us and thus conspicuous adherence is the rule rather than the exception. Take fashion, for example. Because these standards change within our lifetime we can clearly see that these are not based on some set of timeless criteria. It is obvious that they have no particular rational basis (other than to wear warmer clothing when it is cold and cooler when it is hot). And yet, Lord forbid you violate these subjective rules. I once owned a lime-green leisure suit with which I wore a brightly colored floral shirt and platform shoes. Needless to say, it is not part of my current wardrobe. In fact, I find it difficult to even look at pictures of me from the 1970s (and my daughters were very shocked to see photographs of their dad with hair down to his shoulders!). But it is not just me. There would most definitely be social and professional consequences if I suddenly decided to dress as I did back in high school. People would frankly avoid me for my decision to flout a rule of behavior for which there is no rational basis whatsoever and which had been perfectly acceptable in an earlier decade. I might be the very same person, but I would lose status and power, and that is what ceremony is all about.

By contrast, instrumentally warranted behavior is goal-oriented and experimental. Correctness is a function of one's success in achieving the end in question. Such actions are not culturally relative and may be deduced without knowledge of social norms, although information about available technology is necessary. For example, say the goal is dental health. What is the best way to keep your teeth from falling out? Brushing them to remove food and bacteria is a useful method whether you are in modern-day Costa Rica or ancient Rome. Note that this is goal-oriented in the sense that it is not the act of brushing, per se, that is important to you. As such, you will be willing to try different methods. If science develops a new and easier means of maintaining dental hygiene, you would be happy to stop brushing and adopt this new technique. This is typical of instrumentally sanctioned behaviors. Theirs is the logic of trial and error and they are driven by science and technology, not fashion. Even though I do not wear my lime-green leisure suit any more, I still brush my teeth – albeit with a more technologically advanced tooth brush!

The basic aim of Institutionalist research is to determine by which value set an economy is primarily driven. Are behaviors dominated by ceremony such that people generally engage in acts related to status and the creation of invidious distinctions (the subjective determination that one group is superior to another – racism and sexism, for example)? Or is goal-oriented problem solving more common? Here is the true key to the economy, for the former impedes progress while the latter encourages it. The typical approach in such analyses involves pattern modeling and storytelling. This requires studying history and culture to develop internally consistent explanations of behavioral patterns. Note that individual motivations, like utility or profit maximization, are not the object. It would be helpful to know these, but, realistically speaking, how likely is it that we will discover these? Furthermore, the rules of behavior are far more revealing. Take, for example, the situation of walking in on a group of people playing cards. In trying to follow their actions, which is more useful: knowing why they are playing (to win, for comradery, to get out of the house, and so on) or which game it is? Both would be wonderful, but if you can only have one it is an easy choice. This is how Institutionalists view their research. They are trying to figure out what game is being played. What is the object and what are the rules? Note that under this approach, market economies are simply one particular set of rules. Institutionalist economic analysis is much broader.

Institutionalists recognize that there are some obvious problems associated with such a method of analysis. To begin, can one not argue that some ceremonial behaviors are, indeed, oriented toward solving a "problem?" It is certainly true that racist Southerners believed that they had an issue that required resolution. How useful is this analysis if one can use it to argue that the systematic and violent oppression of Americans with darker skin is instrumental? To avoid this, Institutionalists are rather specific regarding what qualifies. Instrumentality is necessarily limited to what they call democratic problem solving, or the extension and enhancement of the life process for the community. Genocide, oppression, discrimination, and so on are thereby expressly excluded. Instrumentality is about raising the standard of living of the average citizen; the goal of ceremony, meanwhile, is the arbitrary award and maintenance of status, power, and privilege.

This still does not give us a set of unambiguously defined analytical concepts and rules that we may apply to an economy to quickly determine whether it is driven by ceremony or instrumentality, but Institutionalists are aware of this. It is hard and contentious work sifting through the value structure of a culture and they make no apology for this. At least such arguments, they say, are focused on the real issues and not on relative trivialities like fiscal policy or tariff rates. At some level the latter are certainly of interest, but they do not hold the key to growth and prosperity (particularly when they, too, are actually driven by the social system). The ceremonial-instrumental dichotomy does.

Incidentally, one highly formal method that has been embraced by Institutionalists is System Dynamics analysis (Sterman 2000). It is essentially a form of computer simulation of social systems created by MIT engineering professor Jay Forrester, but it is far more than just a programming approach. Forrester and his followers have forwarded a number of theories regarding the operation of economies, natural environments, business enterprises, and so on, each of which has tended to be very consistent with Institutionalist analysis. While its use is not yet widespread, there is a strong sense that it may represent a useful means of organizing studies based on the importance of the ceremonial-instrumental dichotomy (Radzicki 1988).

APPLICATION

Because it can be very difficult to imagine these concepts in operation (especially for the traditionally trained economist), an example may be helpful. Perhaps the easiest research to understand is that dealing with developing economies. For example, Institutionalist Dilmus James asks the question, why, despite the fact that Latin American countries unquestionably devoted more resources to technology since the 1960s, had they not achieved any marked progress in terms of development (James 1996)? Should they not, according to the orthodox economic perspective, have found that the increasing ratio of capital to labor resulted in higher growth and standards of living? And yet they had not.

To James, the answer is a function of "inadequate institutions" (James 1996, p. 155). Breaking down the specifics of the value and incentive structures in these nations reveals that, despite a superficial shift toward problem solving and the logic of technology, their societies are instead dominated by status, invidious distinction, and conspicuous consumption. A great deal of this can be traced to the extremely unequal distributions of income and wealth that exist (the deeper reasons for which will be addressed in a moment). As a consequence, power is concentrated in the hands of a very few. Little surprise, then, that extension and enhancement of the life process of the community is not the dominant activity. Instead, the social elites employ the available resources to solidify their position and demonstrate to others how successful they are. Thus, Latin American universities may purchase cutting-edge scientific equipment for which they do not really have a use when what the average citizen needs is far more basic and desperate. The acquisition had nothing to do with the community in general, it was an act of conspicuous consumption on the parts of those in power. It was meant to impress and intimidate others by imitating the consumption patterns of universities in more wealthy nations. This is also why there is more money in being an administrator than a scientist, that projects often have only sufficient funding for the purchase of technical equipment and very little for operation, and that multiple institutions may purchase the same unnecessary equipment. This is not about solving problems, it is about status – it is ceremonial. No amount of World Bank aid, debt forgiveness, or privatization will change this.

This begs the question of whence the tremendous inequities arose in the first place. While a good Institutionalist study would avoid generalizing across all of Latin America, the quick and easy answer here is ethnic. Those who own are typically of Spanish and Portuguese descent; those who do not are Mayan, Aztec, Incan, and so on – the indigenous populations of those modern nations. From the beginning of European colonization, there was a concerted and deliberate attempt to dominate those who inhabited these regions – behavior driven by ceremonial values. This, according to Institutionalists, is the real explanation. Focusing on financial flows, fiscal policy, government budgets, privatization, investment, or savings rates will never shed any real light on what has kept Latin America from development. Rather, they detract our attention from the real issues and offers false precision and spurious correlations in the place of true enlightenment. Once the general orientation of economic activity is shifted toward instrumentality, then we can focus on what interest rates should be.

METHOD

As suggested above, Institutionalists place a great deal of emphasis on description. This is because they do not assume, as in some other schools of thought, that economic behavior is standard across cultures and time. To them, it is no more instinctive than religion, politics, or kinship patterns. This is not to say that there may not be commonalities, but these are to be discovered and not assumed. Thus, an important step in any Institutionalist study is the examination of the social and historical roots of the phenomenon in question. From these, they derive the rules of the game (rules of behavior in that society), which they then study to see which they would categorize as ceremonial and which as instrumental.

Institutionalists believe that, as argued in the card game example, learning the rules of the game is not only more important than knowing agents' motivations, it is actually a more reasonable goal. Reasons for playing may vary widely but, regardless of why they are at the table, in poker three-of-a-kind beats a pair – period. Transferring the analogy to capitalism, a business owner need not be concerned with profit as their personal goal (as assumed in Neoclassicism). It could be that they just enjoy interacting with their customers. BUT, under capitalism, profit is a rule. If your enterprise does not generate greater revenue than expenditures, it must shut down. Hence, everyone is forced, regardless of personal feelings, to earn a profit because of the manner in which our system is organized.

In addition, Institutionalist research sees the economy as simply part of the larger social system. It must be consistent with other social rules and beliefs for them to exist together and the economy will reflect the larger set of values. That said, economies and cultures evolve. This evolution is path-dependent in the sense that past events and human actions create the future. But there is no assumption, as under Marxism, that we will witness some specific, unalterable pattern or that we can expect progression and not regression. This is yet another reason that Institutionalists place heavy emphasis on description: knowing how the US economy worked in 1800 does not guarantee that we know how it worked in 2000.

Note that while Institutionalists are not flatly against building mathematical models, they insist that these must be a means rather than an end. That said, the range of variables assumed to be relevant in the typical Institutionalist study is such that it is often extremely difficult to formalize in the manner necessary to express economic behaviors in equation form. System Dynamics has garnered some attention because its underlying philosophy is similar to that of Institutionalism in that it assumes that social systems are holistic and evolutionary and marked by path-dependent change. It is very flexible, but also complex and it requires specialized software. Thus, while it has been used in some limited applications, it has not become widespread.

VIEWS OF HUMAN NATURE AND JUSTICE

One of the key premises of Institutionalism is that humans are first and foremost social animals. They naturally live in groups in the same manner as lions, hyenas, and chimpanzees. A major part of their identification with the larger group is some set of shared beliefs which, even when they seem ludicrous and arbitrary to others, are viewed as sacrosanct to those within the tribe. This is not to say that there are not pragmatic and utilitarian values, but many are not. Furthermore, *Homo sapiens* want to be considered upstanding members of their social group and thus seek status, sometimes at the expense of others. The latter particularly concerns Institutionalists and one of their primary concerns with respect to justice is the existence of exploitative behavior in society. An economy is fair when it is oriented toward devising pragmatic solutions to the physical and emotional needs of those within the community, not enforcing arbitrary codes of behavior that enrich some by impoverishing others.

STANDARDS

Primary

As has been emphasized above, the social nature of human economic behavior is absolutely central to Institutionalist analysis. Someone arguing otherwise is not an Institutionalist. Likewise, the beliefs that economies are embedded in the rest of society and that they evolve are core. Meanwhile, one will not find any Institutionalist analysis that assumes that the economy automatically tends toward full employment, that agents are completely rational or in possession of full information, or that capitalism is natural. Markets are just one of many tools we can use to achieve instrumental ends.

Secondary

One may, however, find Institutionalists who employ mathematical models and those who reject them. In addition, there are those who think that Institutionalists should openly judge the value structures of societies and others who believe that the fact that we are just as much a product of our own prejudices as those we are studying makes this tricky, at best. Although much of the research on contemporary economies focuses on flaws in the capitalist system, one is nevertheless free in Institutionalism to argue that the market does things well. It is a tool and as such its correctness is a function of the problem at hand.

Something that is noteworthy in Institutionalism is the widespread acceptance of what is to a large extent a different school of thought: Post Keynesianism. Despite the fact that Keynes's work arose independently of their own, many Institutionalists immediately embraced it and in a form that was much more consistent with his original intent. This is not altogether surprising given that Keynes's self-conscious struggle to get his reader to "escape from habitual modes of thought and expression" was unnecessary when it came to Institutionalists. They had already rejected many of the tenets of Neoclassicism that, in the opinion of Keynes and the Institutionalists, created the difficulty mainstream economists had in explaining the Great Depression. The modern-day result of this fact is that the main Institutionalist journal, the *Journal of Economic Issues*, welcomes submissions coming from a Post Keynesian perspective and many Institutionalists also describe themselves as Post Keynesians.

Popular themes in Institutionalist research include economic crisis, the role of culture in economies, and gender issues. That said, the nature of this school of thought is such that a wide variety of topics, from sustainability to pedagogy, is addressed.

CONTEMPORARY ACTIVITIES

There are two main Institutionalist associations, the Association for Institutional Thought (AFIT) and the Association for Evolutionary Economics (AFEE). Both meet annually, the former as a part of the Western Social Science Association (WSSA) and the latter in conjunction with the American Economics Association (AEA). Because AFIT is a large part of

WSSA, they tend to have much more control over their conference. AFEE has found its participation in AEA to be increasingly constrained over the years, including reductions in the number of sessions they are permitted to host. But AFEE is important both because their meetings take place within the much larger annual ones where the primary job market is hosted and they sponsor the main Institutionalist journal, the *Journal of Economic Issues.*

CRITICISMS

The most common attack on Institutionalism is that it is all description and no theory or modeling. How can it truly be a scholarly analysis if you are not identifying generalities and specifying relationships among the various phenomena? While it is quite true that Mars is different from Saturn, which is different from Earth, for example, we cannot expect to understand planets if we leave it there. Our job as scientists is to dig deeper and find out what these have in common and what makes them unique. What Institutionalists practice is uncontrolled speculation where anything goes and laundry lists of individual characteristics substitute for laws of behavior derived from careful deduction.

The other main criticism is that, even if what Institutionalists do is sound research, it is not economics. Study of social relations, power, and cultural mores may well be fascinating and useful, but it is the purview of sociology, anthropology, or history. Economists study prices, markets, and marginal decision making.

FINAL REJOINDER

Institutionalists contend, first, that they *are* developing models and theories, it is just that those trained in other approaches are unfamiliar with their methods. And they do, in fact, believe that very important generalities exist across economies. But these exist with respect to ceremonial and instrumental valuing, the embeddedness of economies in larger social systems, and the centrality of culture and evolution in human behavior. These are the key issues in all economic research. What Neoclassicals see as the common factors are really just flawed observations from their own culture that they then project onto others. This bias is not intentional but, Institutionalists say, a result of exactly what they have been arguing all along: humans think of the behavior of their own tribe as right and natural. This is a tendency for any researcher, be they Neoclassical, Institutionalist, Marxist, or whatever. The problem is that the Neoclassicals are completely unaware that they are committing such an error, while Institutionalists, though not immune, stand guard against it.

With respect to their research not being economics, Institutionalists argue that, to the contrary, they are actually focusing on the issues that truly matter. Whether the money supply should rise by 3 or 5 percent obviously has some significance at a lower level, but in general it is no more important than what kind of weapon Lee Harvey Oswald used to kill President Kennedy. It is not a question without interest, but it is not what makes the incident a watershed event in US history. What we need to study in economics is not simply narrow policy choices within Western market economies. We need to know how these systems evolved, what values justify them, what cultural myths sustain them, how people in them fare, and so on. Capitalism itself is not natural and cannot, therefore, be taken for granted.

FURTHER READING

Thorstein Veblen's *The Theory of the Leisure Class* (1899) remains a classic work by the founder of Institutionalism. In it, he made a scathing attack on the US economy, essentially arguing that the ruling class engaged in conspicuous consumption (a term he coined) on the backs of the industry of the lower classes. Clarence Ayres's *The Theory of Economic Progress* (1944) takes a later and more comprehensive view and is very easy to read. The main Institutionalist journal, the *Journal of Economic Issues*, published two volumes designed as an introduction to their paradigm and these were republished in book form (Tool 1988). The prolific writings of John Kenneth Galbraith represent a Veblenian analysis of the US economy in the mid to late twentieth century and are intended for a general audience. Last, reference to the suggested reading in the chapter on Post Keynesianism might also be of use given that a great many Post Keynesians also consider themselves Institutionalists.

NOTES

1. And even when someone appears to be rejecting widely held values, they are typically copying some behavioral type already established in their culture.
2. It is possible, incidentally, for a ceremonial behavior to have had a more rational, instrumental basis in the past.

REFERENCES

Ayres, C.E. (1944), *The Theory of Economic Progress*, Chapel Hill, NC: University of North Carolina Press.

Bush, P.D. (1987), "The theory of institutional change," *Journal of Economic Issues*, **21** (3), 1075–116.

James, D. (1996), "Technology and third world development," in J. Adams and A. Scaperlanda (eds), *The Institutional Economics of the International Economy*, Boston, MA: Kluwer Academic Publisher, pp. 143–56.

Mayhew, A. (1987), "The beginnings of institutionalism," *Journal of Economic Issues*, **21** (3), 971–98.

Radzicki, M.J. (1988), "Institutional dynamics: an extension of the institutionalist approach to socioeconomic analysis," *Journal of Economic Issues*, **22** (3), 633–66.

Sterman, J.D. (2000), *Business Dynamics: Systems Thinking and Modeling for a Complex World*, Boston, MA: McGraw-Hill Higher Education.

Tool, M.R. (1988), *Evolutionary Economics*, Armonk, NY: M.E. Sharpe.

Veblen, T. (1899), *The Theory of the Leisure Class*, New York: A.M. Kelley.

8. New Institutionalism

The last chapter presented a school of thought premised on the idea that culture is the basic building block for understanding economic behavior. This stands in stark contrast to the individualistic approaches of the Neoclassical and Austrian schools and leads to an analysis that focuses on institutions and patterns of behavior rather than personal motivations and rationality. But are these approaches mutually exclusive or might some combination be possible? New Institutionalism believes that the answer is the latter. While it retains a Neoclassical core (with some elements of Austrianism), it includes a role for institutions. The basic idea is that though we are still studying scarcity and choice, we cannot assume complete information or strict rationality. Transactions costs and uncertainties exist in the economy and institutions are social constructs that can reduce – or add to – the associated costs.

Similar to the argument made in the last chapter, institutions are seen as akin to rules of the game. They include formal and informal regulations plus an enforcement mechanism. Someone's place of work may have a dress code, for example. It limits employees' choices, it may be expressed explicitly (in the form of written guidelines) or implicitly (everyone just knows), and there are rewards for compliance and sanctions for rule breakers. The business itself, however, is not an institution but an organization, or a set of individuals with a common purpose. A university is an organization, too, the common purpose being the creation and dissemination of knowledge. Many institutions exist within the university, including, for example, the process by which one earns tenure. There are written and unwritten rules and an enforcement mechanism. Institutions may be quite obvious or it may require significant study to reveal them. In any event, the focal point of New Institutionalism is the institution, not the organization.

Some institutions are quite helpful because they reduce our transactions costs. For example, let us say that you have a share of stock to sell but that no brokers exist. In that case, you will have to take it upon yourself to find a means of determining who might be interested in acquiring stock, advertising to them that you have a share for sale, monitoring their offers, indicating to whom you are selling it, collecting payment, and transferring ownership. That would be expensive and time-consuming. So, you are willing to submit to the rules of a brokerage house and the government agency that regulates their activities, plus pay a fee, in order to a make it easier to sell your share of stock. Brokering can thus be a beneficial institution that reduces transactions costs.

The situation is not always so rosy, however (Vardy 2010). Say in the brokerage example that the government regulators demanded bribes to approve transactions. This would actually add to the cost of doing business rather than lowering it. In this instance, people would certainly not choose to submit to this, but the power structure may be such that they have no choice. This discourages economic activity and New Institutionalists see underdevelopment as a function of issues like this.

Whether or not useful institutions survive and harmful ones die is dependent on a number of factors. First, relative prices may play a role. This does not mean prices in the traditional sense, but in the context of the transactions cost reduction represented by the institution. *Ceteris paribus*, those that reduce costs most are preferred and are more likely to survive; those that do not may fall into misuse and die. But the story is not that simple, for power, ideology, and path dependence also play a role. With respect to the first, it is sometimes true that those with the most power to change the rules are also the ones with the least incentive to do so. In the case of the government officials above, they have no reason to stop charging bribes. If they are the ones best positioned to alter the rules, then the rules will not change. But if the customers or brokers have an economic or political means of affecting change, then the institution may evolve. Ideology also plays a role. *Homo sapiens* do not interact with "reality," but their impression thereof. They operate with a mental model that tells them how the world works and where they fit into it. An important part of this is the individual's ideology: their ideals, taboos, sense of justice, values, and so on. These are derived from the larger society and determine the conditions under which the formation and evolution of institutions takes place. Many aspects of Medieval Catholicism clashed with and hindered the development of capitalism; Japanese attitudes toward the body have limited the number of organ transplant surgeries there; some religious doctrines condemn women to lower status; and so on. Such ideological stances can be very powerful and they act to enhance or inhibit economic development. New Institutionalists also believe that path dependence must be considered. History is important. A common example is the QWERTY keyboard. This layout is intentionally awkward because the goal was to slow typists as they used early and easily jammed typewriters. QWERTY accomplishes this by spreading out the most commonly used letters rather than concentrating them. As technology has made the jamming issue moot, one would think that the changing structure of the implicit prices would mean that a more efficient layout would be adopted. Not, so, because so many people had already been trained (and continue to be trained) on QWERTY. The perceived cost of shifting has been considered too high to move to what everyone agrees would be a more efficient arrangement.

In their study of the issues outlined above, New Institutionalists are often led to examine the legal structure of societies and their property rights institutions. This is so because implicit in their analysis is the assumption that market-based exchange is generally superior to other forms of economic organization in fostering development. They believe that one of the reasons for the rapid technological growth of the West was that their institutions encouraged the evolution of capitalism, which then created incentives and opportunities not available in other systems. Within this context, a key question is how much control (as granted by formal and informal institutions) individuals have over all forms of property. One is more likely, they argue, to develop a more profitable means of growing potatoes when the lion's share of the benefit will accrue to you. A serf on a medieval manor, a member of a communal farm, or a slave has much less incentive and therefore such systems are less likely to generate economic development.

Unfortunately, say New Institutionalists, history tells us that vested interest and path dependence are, more often than not, successful in blocking the development of more efficient institutions. People will embrace inefficiency if doing so allows them to remain true to their ideology. When tremendous inequities exist in a culture, those at the top of the hierarchy are both those most able to effect change and the ones least likely to want it. And if a society has evolved with a land tenure system that discourages efficient farming techniques, it is very difficult to universally adopt a new one even if everyone can see the benefit. In fact, all these impediments are so difficult to overcome that New Institutionalists believe that efficient institutional change is rare.

APPLICATION: THE FINANCIAL CRISES OF 1763 AND 2007–08

For obvious reasons, economic history is a popular research topic for New Institutionalists (as is economic development). While to some extent this is motivated simply by curiosity, it is also true that they believe that studies of the past offer lessons for the present. Take, for example,

Stephen Quinn and William Roberds's study of the financial crisis of 1763 (Quinn and Roberds 2012). This paper focuses on the institution of merchant banking, wherein banks earn income by guaranteeing borrowers' debts. For example, say Merchant A wants to purchase goods on credit from Merchant B. Merchant B must trust that Merchant A will pay in a timely manner. If not, either the transaction will not take place or Merchant A will be charged a higher price. This is particularly problematic if Merchant A is not well known or is relatively small or new. In addition, this requires Merchant B to specialize in both the production of the goods and services they sell and the evaluation of the creditworthiness of their customers.

But, if Merchant A borrows from a bank and Merchant B is paid immediately with bank credit, then two beneficial things happen:

1. The risk that Merchant A defaults is shifted from Merchant B to the bank, an entity that is presumably better suited to evaluating and managing this.
2. While Merchant B must still worry that the bank may default, the bank spends a great deal of effort both determining the viability of those to whom it lends and in developing a reputation for reliability; this is therefore generally preferable to the risk associated with dealing directly with Merchant A.

In this manner, transactions costs have been reduced.

Amsterdam was an important source of such services in the late eighteenth century. During the Seven Years' War (1756 to 1763), a great deal of extra business was generated for the bankers as they financed both governments and war-related businesses. The rising prices created by shortages helped firms earn income that allowed them to repay debt with relative ease. In such an environment, it was very tempting for banks to make an increasing volume of loans because the more money you loan, the more interest you earn – assuming the borrower repays.

But when the war ended, so did the extra revenues. The fact that the banks financed their own operations via short-term borrowing created a very fragile situation. If you have no debt and experience a decline in income, it is possible that you may be able to weather the bad times by cutting back on expenditures. Those heavily indebted, however, have very few options in that regard. Their creditors expect – in fact, need, since they are often debtors themselves – the regular payments you promised. When that flow is interrupted, bankruptcy may not be far behind. Given the interlocking nature of debts, default can spread very quickly from banks to firms and back again.

This is precisely what happened in 1763. Prices fell dramatically after the war and the unlucky first victim was Gebroeders de Neufville, a new bank whose loans, say Quinn and Roberds, did not appear to be significantly riskier than anyone else's. Furthermore, the default that set things into motion was actually from one of Neufville's smaller accounts. However, the impact on the bank's own large weekly borrowing needs was decisive. This was the first in a series of events that led to a number of bank and merchant failures and economic disaster for Amsterdam and beyond.

There are, argue Quinn and Roberds, a number of parallels with the events of 2007–08. In the more recent case, a boom in housing prices seemed to make mortgages and mortgage-backed derivatives a no-lose proposition. Just as with the inflated prices of the Seven Years' War, this led to a sharp increase in financial market activity and a reduction in the caution exercised by lenders. But after the bubble burst, the result was the same as it had been more than two centuries earlier. When Lehman Brothers failed – again, a firm whose operations did not appear to be particularly risky compared to others – this sent shock waves through the financial community. The interconnectedness of the debt structure meant that defaults spread quickly and the overall level of economic activity declined substantially.

What is most instructive, say Quinn and Roberds, is the comparison of regulators' response. In both instances, governments made plentiful supplies of liquidity available, which calmed fears and slowed the rate of default. In 1763, however, banks were permitted to fail; in 2007, most were rescued. Quinn and Roberds consider these differences and run a number of simulations that look at other policy choices. In general, they conclude that modern relief efforts were somewhat more successful. This, they say, was because policy makers offered liquidity not just domestically, but across national borders. Thus, they use this analysis not only to further our understanding of 1763, but to offer lessons for 2007 and beyond. Furthermore, the core focal point of their analysis was the institution of merchant banking and how it can serve to subtract from or add to transactions costs.

Before leaving this section, note the similarity between some of the New Institutionalist premises and those of the Austrians. They agree, for example, that economic agents must work with limited information and that they may struggle to determine which choice is best for them. They see markets as a key institution in solving this problem. And both perspectives also believe that market-based economies hold the greatest promise of development. New Institutionalists, however, place a much greater emphasis on the role of institutions and culture. Still, there has been some cross-fertilization.

METHOD

Because it derives from several disparate traditions, the New Institutionalist method is a bit of a hybrid. On the one hand, it retains the Austrian/Neoclassical focus on the individual, scarcity, and choice. On the other, not only do institutions matter, but so do power, culture, ideology, and history. Thus, despite other similarities, New Institutionalists generally do not engage in the a priori or as-if arguments typical of Austrians and Neoclassicals or, if they do, it is simply as a first step to lay out some behavioral proclivities. Like the Institutionalists of the previous chapter, New Institutionalists examine specific institutional structures, their origins, their evolution, and the nature of the societies in which they are found. Unlike Institutionalists, they still see humans as rational after some fashion and as the ultimate forces of change. Thus, consistent with the Austrians, they believe that individuals, not institutions, act and they therefore retain the former as the basic unit of analysis.

VIEWS OF HUMAN NATURE AND JUSTICE

Because of their Neo-Austrian focus on the individual, they take a similar view of human nature. Individuals, though impacted by institutions, are the true agents of change in society. They create the institutions that then reduce or increase transactions costs. People are guided by self-interest and they are quasi-rational, but they are naturally limited in the latter by their finite cognitive abilities and the always-insufficient amount of information available.

Also like the Austrians, New Institutionalists view justice as outcomes that reflect the collective preferences of humans. Markets are not perfect, but they are the best means of making output and prices reflect this. Historically, it has been those countries that embraced market exchange that have created incentives that generated the greatest economic development. They got the institutions right.

STANDARDS

Primary

First and foremost is the contention that institutions matter. Without such a premise it would hardly be New Institutionalist economics. It is universally believed that the formal and informal rules of an economic unit are decisive in determining its success. Within that context, human beings are viewed as operating with limited cognitive abilities and incomplete information, both of which contribute to the existence of transactions costs. But New Institutionalism retains its Neoclassical core in that it is seen as studying scarcity and choice.

Secondary

Some New Institutionalist economists self-consciously trace their tradition through the founders of the Institutionalist tradition discussed in the previous chapter. For example, Oliver Williamson (2000) cites the work of Institutionalists John Commons and Wesley Clair Mitchell in a very positive light. On the other hand, others, like Nobel Laureate Douglass North, deny that any such connection exists except by coincidence (Dugger 1995; ironically, Dugger argues that North's work actually comes closer to Institutionalism than Williamson's). The extent to which formal, mathematical modeling is embraced varies. Those dubbed the New New Institutionalists by Peter Spiegler and William Milberg make a point of using "hyper-reductive mathematical models to represent these institutions as a means of explaining them" (Spiegler and Milberg 2009, p. 293). Their work still includes descriptive analyses of the phenomena in question, but the formal framework is considered to be the driving force. Others see such techniques as supplemental, with the historical and institutional descriptions as the key element. Common themes in New Institutionalist literature include property rights, law, the historical evolution of institutions, and development. Entering such debates may enhance your chance of publication but is not, of course, absolutely necessary.

CONTEMPORARY ACTIVITIES

The main organization for New Institutionalists is the International Society for New Institutional Economics (http://www.isnie.org/). They hold an annual international conference and their website includes a list of readings for those interested in New Institutionalist economics. They also provide access to current job openings where the hiring institution may be open to their approach. While there is no journal devoted to New Institutionalist research, their website maintains an automated list of related work. This school of thought is, in general, relatively young and still maturing and growing.

CRITICISMS

Those coming from more traditional approaches are likely to argue that, as with the school of thought covered in the last chapter, New Institutionalism is not really economics. The issues discussed are of interest, but they are more properly the object of study of historians and sociologists. Perhaps ironically, Institutionalists also object to a number of aspects of New Institutionalism (while at the same time praising others). Most fundamentally, they argue that institutions exist not because of transactions costs and uncertainties, but because *Homo sapiens* are social animals. Even if people had complete information and were lightning-quick calculators of pain and pleasure, they would nevertheless live in packs because that is our nature. A core element of these packs is a set of shared beliefs, including behavioral norms. Therefore, institutions, including ideology, arise from our natural desire to be a member of a social group. Speaking of which, they would argue that New Institutionalism's bias toward market-based solutions is not a result of dispassionate analysis, but really an unconscious reflection of the economists' own ideologies. The market is no more than one tool in our kit. New Institutionalism, say Institutionalists, needs to let go of these last vestiges of Neoclassicism.

FINAL REJOINDER

To the first criticism, the New Institutionalists (like the Institutionalists) would respond that if laying out the specific conditions under which the financial crisis of 1763 took place is not economics, then what is it? We of course have a set of common premises guiding our analyses of each period, but there are sufficient differences between what happened 250 years ago and in 2007 to warrant a more contextual analysis. Indeed, there is no other way to explain these two events.

To the Institutionalists, they would say that the preference for market solutions is most certainly not an ideological bias. The evidence that such systems generate more efficient outcomes is overwhelming. The vast gulf between the post-colonial development of North and South America, for example, is due to differences in property rights and other legal and informal institutions that created a very different set of incentives and power structures. Generally speaking, where capitalism was successful, economies grew. With respect to the origin of institutions, New Institutionalists would not deny the social nature of *Homo sapiens*. However, reliance on such a general characterization of the phenomenon provides no guide to how they evolve. The concepts of transactions costs, power, ideology, bounded rationality, and path dependence all offer powerful means of doing so.

FURTHER READING

Perhaps the best starting place for New Institutionalist economics is one of Douglass North's books (1990 or 2005, for example) or one of his survey articles (1991). Or Ronald Coase's (1937) classic work on transactions costs is very interesting and easy to read. Two New Institutionalist websites have extensive reading lists organized by topic. Look under "Resources" on the International Society for New Institutional Economics website (http://www.isnie.org) and under "New Institutional Economics" at the Ronald Coase Institute website (http://www.coase.org).

REFERENCES

Coase, R. (1937), "The nature of the firm," *Economica*, **4**, 386–495.
Dugger, W.M. (1995), "Douglass C. North's new institutionalism," *Journal of Economic Issues*, **29** (2), 453–8.
North, D.C. (1990), *Institutions, Institutional Change, and Economic Performance*, Cambridge: Cambridge University Press.
North, D.C. (1991), "Institutions," *Journal of Economic Perspectives*, **5** (1), 97–112.
North, D.C. (2005), *Understanding the Process of Economic Change*, Princeton, NJ: Princeton University Press.
Quinn, S. and W. Roberds (2012), "Responding to a shadow banking crisis: the lessons of 1763," Federal Reserve Bank of Atlanta Working Paper, available at http://www.frbatlanta.org/documents/news/conferences/12monetary_econ/12monetary_econ_quinn_roberds.pdf (accessed March 17, 2014).
Spiegler, P. and W. Milberg (2009), "The taming of institutions in economics: the rise and methodology of the 'new new institutionalism,'" *Journal of Institutional Economics*, **5** (3), 289–313.
Vardy, F. (2010), "Institutional traps," Vanderbilt University Working Paper, available at http://faculty.haas.berkeley.edu/fvardy/Institutions.pdf (accessed April 4, 2014).
Williamson, O.E. (2000), "The New Institutional economics: taking stock, looking ahead," *Journal of Economic Literature*, **38** (3), 595–613.

9. Feminist economics

Feminist economics is not just economics that considers gender issues; in fact, that is not even necessary. Rather, while it was originally inspired by an attempt to explain the lot of women and though that continues to be a major focus, Feminist economics has evolved into a unique philosophical and analytical approach that can be applied to any issue.

Researchers in this area draw from a number of paradigms. This is so because "the intellectual groundwork was established by scholars working in … neoclassical economics, institutionalist economics, and Marxist political economy" (Barker 2005, p. 2192). And though no community of scholars is completely homogeneous, it should be clear from the earlier chapters that the differences among these approaches can be quite significant! This makes Feminist economics a particularly interesting study, especially in a volume that argues that pluralistic approaches are more likely to generate useful and reliable explanations. No other paradigm in this book reaches more broadly across the spectrum for its inspiration.

ECONOMICS FOR WHAT?

Feminist economics asks some very fundamental questions about our discipline. What, for example, does it mean to practice economics? Is it, as maintained by many in the mainstream, the description of objective facts and the value-free analysis of the way the world is? Or does it require subjective interpretations of what we observe followed by normative recommendations of changes that we believe will improve people's lives? Feminists say the answer is clearly the latter (Hewitson 2010). Even those economists who claim to be doing the former are, in fact, making value judgements. Because there cannot be a view except from a view point, all theories and models are necessarily based on ideological and philosophical assumptions that directly affect their analyses and policy recommendations. Those who argue that economics is a coldly rational institution, slowly replacing ignorance with knowledge, are epistemologically ignorant; it is a social process that is embedded within a particular culture and is therefore subject to all the same biases and limitations as the people conducting it.

Delving deeper, if, as Feminist economists argue, an integral part of doing economics is recommending policy to improve people's lives, then we need a means of measuring economic wellbeing. While economists of every variety would concede that this is a complex question, most would likely point to GDP as a reasonable choice. Defined as the total dollar value of all goods and services produced and sold within a country in a given time period, it is widely considered to be one of the most important measures of aggregate economic activity and a natural focal point for policy recommendations. Raising GDP should, *ceteris paribus*, raise people's happiness.

But herein lies yet another fundamental objection from the Feminist school of thought. While definitions and statistical categories may seem to be neutral constructions, they are most certainly not. How we decide to categorize people, things, and activities is, consistent with the discussion above, value-laden. It reflects what distinctions we think are important and which activities are worthy of study. Take race, for example. This is not a scientific category, but a social one. It classifies people by characteristics that are significant only because a particular society has decided they are. Ironically, this subjectivity does not make race un-important. Quite the opposite, such categorizations operate to define reality for us. For good or bad, they say who you are, determine how others view you, and define your role in society.

Not surprisingly, Feminists see gender classifications in this same light. What we decide is feminine or masculine is socially constructed and varies across time and space. Even the categories themselves vary, as straight, gay, lesbian, bisexual, and transgendered are gaining acceptance over the simple binary male-female. And yet, despite their lack of scientific validity, these definitions play a crucial role in how we live our lives and in how we view ourselves and others. They reflect and reinforce social roles and power relationships.

The subjectivity and cultural relativity of definitions like race and gender is easy to see. What is more subtle is the impact of abstract theoretical constructs like GDP. Since we cannot look at everything at once, these offer important focal points. But because such categories do not exist in nature, they, too, are reflective of social choices. The phenomena they illuminate are those we deem sufficiently important to expend resources in studying. Anything we deem uninteresting or insignificant goes uncounted. With that in mind, consider the following with respect to GDP: our most popular measure of economic activity and wellbeing totally ignores non-market acts like home management and child rearing that are often the near-exclusive domain of women.[1] This is despite the fact that "unpaid labor in the home – caring labor – is of major significance to the economy. It underpins the ability of people to provide labor to the paid economy and is an essential component of the development of future citizens, workers, and taxpayers" (Hewitson 2003, p. 266). This is not, according to Feminist economists, a minor oversight that could be corrected with a footnote or dummy variable, but a reflection of a deep-seated cultural bias. It is rooted in the belief that activities traditionally undertaken by men are more important than those performed by women.

The importance of this goes beyond economic theory. Consider the impact of using GDP as the gauge of prosperity. This implies, for example, that it is more socially valuable for a single mother (or father) to take a low-wage, dead-end job than concentrate on the extremely hard work of teaching a child discipline, self-worth, and respect for others. Indeed, those opting for the latter (particularly when they fall into certain racial categories) may be condemned as parasites and accused of living off the labor of others. This characterization has affected policy. In the United States, for example, one of the reasons public assistance has become increasing difficult to obtain since the 1980s is the widespread belief that home work is less valuable than market work. Measures like GDP mean that economic theory operates to support this perspective.

The definition of GDP is particularly problematic in developing nations where the power differential between men and women is often the greatest. Not only may attempts to raise the nation's GDP pull men away from those aspects of home management and child-rearing jobs where they had once assisted (thus reducing the quantity and quality of those activities), but it is unlikely that women will be permitted to share in the income and property earned as a result of the market-based activities. Thus, while we pat ourselves on the back for the wonderful job we have done in raising GDP in the developing world, women are often finding themselves in worse shape than when we started. A different definition of economic wellbeing might well lead to different policies and results.

Many economists might interject here that while caring labor is obviously important, the problem is that it is more properly the study of sociologists and social workers. It fails a primary standard of behavior, that is, it is not economics. But if our discipline focuses only on market-based activities then we have to concede that the overwhelming majority of human history has no economic significance. Except for trivialities or dubious analogies, our tools of analysis would be useless in studying feudalism, the Roman empire, subsistence farming, or the

Aztecs. Surely no one thinks that is true. Rather, our focus on markets over non-market activity is ideological and cultural, a function of the implicit assumption that what women do is less valuable.

These biases go beyond definitions and statistical categories. The very tools of modern Neoclassical economics are rooted in processes that reflect the social conception of male-ness, such as competition, exploit, and survival of the fittest. In this manner, our discipline becomes one of many means by which we are taught that masculinity is superior to femininity. Nor is its influence minor:

> The discursive power of economics is not to be underestimated. Economics, particularly neoclassical economics (the type of analyses taught in most undergraduate economics courses, extolled in publications such as the *New York Times* and the *Wall Street Journal*, and lauded by national and international politicians and policy makers), is widely considered to be objective, gender neutral, and value free. Its pronouncements are couched in the same terms as natural laws, and the "laws of supply and demand" are accorded the same status as the law of gravity. The scientific status of economics depends crucially on its methods of inquiry: methodological individualism, rational choice theory, and mathematical modeling. (Barker 2005, pp. 2194–5)

These theories, say Feminists, are far from objective, gender neutral, and value-free, but those who benefit from the power relations these theories justify have every reason to argue otherwise. It allows them to offer a supposedly scientific justification for the under-representation of women (and other disadvantaged groups) in certain jobs, the existence of wage differentials, and the inferior status of home or caring work. As it stands, economics is part of the problem, not part of the solution.

Feminist economics is, therefore, an approach that asks us to carefully consider the impact of culture not simply on the economy, but on economics. Science is conducted by people who are members of particular social groups. Those groups have implicit and explicit views of justice, religion, politics, nature, kinship patterns, race, gender, and so on. Feminists argue that all of these (not just the last one) have a major impact on how we do economics. They shape definitions, theories, the manner in which processes are modeled, and so on. And if we disagree with some of the values imported from the broader culture then it may not be enough to tweak the analysis by shifting a curve to the left instead of the right; you might have to change the economics itself.

This is precisely what the Feminists are arguing. They disagree with the inferior status assigned to femininity by society at large and subsequently reflected in economics. Many existing tools of analysis are therefore useless in addressing this inequity because they implicitly embrace it. If we are to improve the lot of those we study, then we have to develop an alternative economics.

PARADIGMATIC APPROACHES TO FEMINIST ECONOMICS

But what that alternative should be varies somewhat and is affected by the school or schools of thought influencing the researcher in question. As mentioned at the opening of this chapter, Feminist economics draws from three disparate groups: Neoclassicism, Marxism, and Institutionalism. While to some extent pluralistic and even interdisciplinary work is encouraged, there are also elements of each of the three that are mutually exclusive. Neoclassicism's focus on the rational individual with independent preferences, for example, clashes at a very fundamental level with Institutionalism's core concepts of culture and values. Thus, while one could draw selectively from Neoclassicism, Marxism, and Institutionalism to build a coherent Feminist alternative to mainstream economics, it would not be possible to simply combine all three. For that reason, this section is divided into three subsections: Neoclassical influences, Marxist influences, and Institutionalist influences. In each, the elements upon which Feminists have drawn will be highlighted. This does not mean that everyone uses all these, but then the general methodology of Feminism is one that encourages creativity and experimentation. By this pluralistic approach they hope to avoid the fundamental errors they perceive in other approaches.

Neoclassical Influences

The majority of economists are Neoclassical and almost everyone was at least trained in this tradition, even if they later chose another route. As explained in Chapter 3, among the core concepts in Neoclassicism are that economic agents are rational and that market systems tend to generate optimal outcomes wherein wages, incomes, and profits are a function of objectively determined contributions to national wealth. It is possible even within Neoclassicism to take issue with these, but as they are the default beliefs one must be prepared to spend considerable time and effort in defending any alternate premises. Such violations of secondary standards of behavior carry considerable risk, especially when one considers that being ostracized from Neoclassicism also means losing out on access to what is by far the largest share of resources in our discipline.

That said, it is very difficult to build a Feminist alternative without rejecting those concepts for they exhibit the very same male biases from which they are trying to escape. To demonstrate the difficulties involved, let us examine the work of someone who tried to explain gender issues without rejecting those premises: Gary Becker (1930–2014). While he was not a Feminist economist, he was a very important and well-known figure in our discipline and the criticisms to which his work is subjected by Feminists are instructive.

Gary Becker's study of the family assumes a standard Neoclassical model, about which he writes in the introduction to *A Treatise on the Family*:

> It [Neoclassical economics] now assumes that individuals maximize their utility from basic preferences that do not change rapidly over time, and that the behavior of different individuals is coordinated by explicit and implicit markets ... This volume uses the assumptions of maximizing behavior, stable preferences, and equilibrium in implicit or explicit markets to provide a systematic analysis of the family. I build on my research during the past decade to analyze the allocation of time to children and to market work, marriage and divorce in polygynous as well as monogamous societies, altruism in addition to selfishness in families, intergenerational mobility, and many other aspects of the family. (Becker 1981, pp. ix–x)

Gary Becker's work is considered classic within Neoclassicism and he earned the 1992 Nobel Prize in Economics "for having extended the domain of microeconomic analysis to a wide range of human behaviour and interaction, including nonmarket behaviour" (Nobel Foundation n.d.).

An example of his Neoclassically based analysis of gender issues is his examination of the differential between men's and women's wages (Becker 1985). He agrees that even taking into account various other factors, one may still be left with a residual between what a male and female worker is paid. But Becker does not assume that discrimination is occurring in the workplace. He argues instead that this same outcome is consistent with (a) increasing returns to investments in human capital; (b) women having the greater responsibility (for whatever reason) for child rearing and home maintenance; and (c) the fact that child rearing and home maintenance are more tiring than leisure. The first says that more time spent at a particular market job raises one's productivity in that employment and, hence, one's wage. If women spend less time than men outside the home, they are logically less skilled. The second and third imply that if men are choosing only between labor and leisure, while women have the added responsibility of home maintenance and child rearing, then women probably have less energy remaining for any market work they may undertake. They therefore voluntarily seek less-demanding, lower-paying work, and any human capital/experience they build up at all (which is already likely to be less than that of husbands) will be in jobs with poor pay and benefits. And this is why men get paid more than women. The freely chosen division of labor in the home creates the economically fair wage differential we observe in the workplace. As he says, "housework responsibilities lower the earnings and affect the jobs of married women by reducing their time in the labor force and discouraging their investment in market human capital" (Becker 1985, p. S55).

But why, say Feminists, should such a gender-based allocation of labor exist in the first place, for this is obviously a key question? One of the possibilities suggested by Becker is that it is based on natural ability and the consequent comparative advantages. Women do home work because they are better at it. Critics argue, however, that he is engaging in circular logic: it is obvious that women are better at housework because they specialize in it, and they specialize in it because they are better at it (see Hewitson 1999, pp. 54–64; the following discussion is based on that passage). Furthermore, this explanation is premised on the idea that all agents have an equal say in how household resources are managed or that everyone is truly free to choose. Therefore, the consequent allocations must be optimal because if they were not, people would not have selected them. Some have openly suggested that this is a result of an arrogant male belief that if they (the men) are happy, then the arrangement must be fair. Even when Becker allows for the possibility that there might be discrimination in the household (that is, men are forcing women into the home maker role), he suggests it is in the best interest of the utility-maximizing husband to make the most efficient choice. Any way you cut it, the allocation of household labor is optimal.

Another criticism raised is that Becker's approach discounts the possibility that home work is marketable. Surely the ability to cook, clean, raise children, and otherwise manage a household is something that could be translated into income? Indeed, there are market equivalents of all of these tasks. Why, then, are even home-bound women not developing saleable skills? That this is not even considered is, they say, further evidence of the masculinist bias of economics.

The bottom line is that it is, according to Feminists, impossible to explain the lot of women using the standard Neoclassical model. The latter was built on the implicit assumption that the status quo was objectively fair and its definitions, theories, and models reflect this. It serves to justify and perpetuate the existing social hierarchy, just as the Divine Right of Kings justified the status of the feudal serf. It is impossible to use the former to emancipate the latter. This is not to say that all of Neoclassicism must be rejected and, indeed, there are Neoclassically inspired Feminist works (Figart and Mutari 1999, p. 335). Concepts like formal and informal markets, maximizing behavior, stable preferences, and equilibrium can be employed, but not without allowing for the possibility of discrimination, power differentials, and suboptimal outcomes. To Feminist economists, the existence of inequities is not an open question but an empirical fact and one that demands explanation.

Marxist Influences

At the end of the day, however, Neoclassicism is poorly equipped to answer the real key question, that is, the ultimate source of the discrimination against women. For that reason, those seeking answers have wandered outside both Neoclassicism and economics. One would think that Marxism might be useful in this regard. After all, while mainstream economics suggests that any outcomes generated by the free market must be fair, one of the core premises of the former is that gross inequities are an inevitable feature of capitalism. And, indeed, this observation is not without merit. However, because Marxism's theory of discrimination arose from different concerns and antedated the Feminist movement, its basis is not gender, but class (Albelda 1997, p. 129). Furthermore, class was hardly a secondary concept for Marx so it cannot be easily subordinated. Not only is it the source of the core injustice in the system, it plays a central role in the contradictions that emerge. One cannot, therefore, simply replace "workers" with "women" and tell the same story. That Feminist issues are often subsumed under class ones is obviously unacceptable to those more concerned with the former. In addition, some Feminists have accused Marxism of some of the same oversights as Neoclassicism. For example:

> Feminists complain, with considerable justice, that Marx's value theory degrades women's domestic labour by categorising it as "useful but unproductive." Useful, because it is essential for the reproduction of the capitalist mode of production itself; unproductive, since it produces neither commodities, nor value, nor surplus value. (Howard and King 1992, p. 281)

Last, just as Neoclassicism employs statistical categories that downplay traditionally female activities, so the very basis of Marxist exploitation theory falls into this same trap because it is based on wage labor and the generation of a surplus that is retained by the capitalist (Albelda 1997, p. 141). By this definition, those not doing wage labor cannot be exploited!

Nevertheless, many Feminists are attracted to Marxist and, more broadly, socialist theory. It does, at least, allow for the existence of oppression, alienation, and significant power differentials in a way that Neoclassicism does not. And just because traditional Marxism is based on class and market transactions does not mean that modern studies must also be. Indeed, a number of Feminists have adopted Marx's historical dialectic as a tool of analysis (Albelda 1997, pp. 142–3). Particularly appealing are the ideas that human behavior is a function of their institutional and material circumstances and that society evolves. Marx's view that humans should be free to control their own destinies and to develop the skills they choose while cooperating with rather than competing against their sibling workers also rings true. Still, the marriage between Marxism and Feminism has been a rocky one (Hartmann 1981).

Institutionalist Influences

What appears to have been a more harmonious combination has been that between Feminism and Institutionalism. This is not surprising given the fact that the founder of the latter, Thorstein Veblen (1857–1929), was deeply interested in gender issues (Miller 1972; Waddoups and Tilman 1992). Recall from Chapter 7 that Institutionalists argue that *Homo sapiens* are social animals and as such they instinctively seek out tribal membership. Membership is a function of shared beliefs, practices, valuation systems, and so on. In terms of the last, Institutionalists argue that two basic evaluative categories exist: ceremonial and instrumental. Ceremonial values are past-binding and oriented toward defining status. Behaviors sanctioned by ceremony derive their legitimacy not from logic or experimentation, but from authority, and they tend to be exploitative in the sense that they encourage actions that expropriate rather than build. Meanwhile, instrumentally warranted behavior is goal-oriented and experimental and is democratically based. Propriety is a function of one's success in achieving the end in question and actions are more commonly associated with industriousness and nurturing. These are reflected in Veblen's writing on gender (note that the "two sets of human activities" referenced below are directly related to ceremony and instrumentality):

> According to Veblen, two sets of human activities and their corresponding values, beliefs, and meanings form the point and counterpoint of human existence. On one hand is male personal exploit and on the other hand is female social industry. Male exploit is aimed at seizure of wealth (ownership), capture of slaves and servants (ownership/marriage) and display of status (conspicuous consumption and conspicuous leisure). Female industry is aimed at production of serviceable items (the instinct of workmanship), care of

children and the infirm (parental bent), and the increase and sharing of arts and crafts (idle curiosity). (Dugger 1994, pp. 3–4)

Thus, modern Institutionalists see their school of thought as offering a more fertile ground for Feminist economics than either of the other two paradigms discussed so far in this chapter. Gender discrimination is not seen as derivative of class, as in Marxism, nor as a function of some unexplained personal taste, as in Neoclassicism. Instead, Institutionalism "emphasizes the role of cultural myth" (Dugger 1994, p. 5). The inferiority of women in our society, they argue, has its roots in our shared cultural beliefs that have been passed from generation to generation and, under most circumstances, accepted without question – even by women. To Institutionalists, sexism is a ceremonial value that creates an invidious distinction: men are more important than women.

According to Veblen, this value originated around 10,000 years ago, as we transitioned from hunter-gatherer societies to permanent settlements with domesticated animals, agriculture, and an increasing number of tools. This created the possibility of a predatory life whereby one group supported itself by taking the food, tools, homes, animals, people, and so on of others. In such societies and in those where they are forced to defend themselves:

> The group divides itself conventionally into a fighting and a peace-keeping class, with a corresponding division of labor. Fighting, together with other work that involves a serious element of exploit, becomes the employment of the able-bodied men; the uneventful everyday work of the group falls to the women and the infirm. (Veblen 1898–99, p. 504)

The reason for the division of labor is simple: men, on average, are physically stronger than women. This does not in and of itself suggest that a value should evolve that implies that women are inferior, but it is not difficult to imagine. Even without the development of predatory lifestyles, brute strength favors men.

Institutionalists believe that this invidious distinction survived primitive society – indeed, those in power had little incentive to see it end. Even today, "male" is the default standard while "female" is an inferior version of male. William Dugger writes of women:

> If she likes to climb trees when a girl, it is because she is a "tomboy." If a boy likes to climb trees, no questions are asked and no answers must be given. While a young man who likes to paint nude women has no explaining to do, a young woman who likes to paint nude men has quite a lot of explaining to do – she must explain why she is not merely sublimating her alleged desire to be a man. While a young man struggling to advance his professional career

has no explaining to do, a young woman doing the same has quite a lot of explaining to do – she must explain why she is putting off having children. And so on, and on. (Dugger 1994, p. 5)

This, say Institutionalists, is the reason women find themselves with lower wages and less control over family assets, excluded from positions of economic power, and so on. Traditionally, female-dominated jobs earn less respect and while women in "male" jobs are sometimes looked upon as having been successful despite their gender, men in "women's" jobs are viewed with suspicion. As Veblen wrote over 100 years ago:

One of the early consequences of this deprecation of infirmity is a tabu on women and on women's employments. In the apprehension of the archaic, animistic barbarian, infirmity is infectious. The infection may work its mischievous effect both by sympathetic influence and by transfusion. Therefore it is well for the able-bodied man who is mindful of his virility to shun all undue contact and conversation with the weaker sex and to avoid all contamination with the employments that are characteristic of the sex. Even the habitual food of women should not be eaten by men, lest their force be thereby impaired. The injunction against womanly employments and foods and against intercourse with women applies with especial rigor during the season of preparation for any work of manly exploit, such as a great hunt or a warlike raid, or induction into some manly dignity or society or mystery. Illustrations of this seasonal tabu abound in the early history of all peoples that have had a warlike or barbarian past. (Veblen 1898–99, p. 504)

Although Veblen was hopeful that this value was breaking down, Institutionalists say that elements of these taboos are still evident today. Institutionalism thereby offers Feminism a framework within which to understand the social status of women.

METHOD

A key starting point for Feminist methodology is their contention that economics is not and cannot be value-free. Science is always embedded in the larger culture such that those conducting it are affected by the values they carry with them. The consequent masculinist bias of economics has meant that our discipline operates as an intellectual justification for the inferior status of women (and other disadvantaged groups). This is not specific to economics, but a function of broader social values. Feminist researchers are therefore very sensitive to the fact that all definitions, models, and theories are value-laden. This is unavoidable, but by openly recognizing this we become more cognizant of the strengths and weaknesses of our work and are thus able to create more realistic analyses.

Within that general context, Feminist economists draw from a number of intellectual traditions both in economics and beyond in undertaking their studies. They embrace this pluralistic approach as consistent with the broader philosophy above. In addition, the fact that existing economic schools of thought have been impacted by the very biases Feminists hope to avoid means that, as a practical matter, one is forced to pick and choose among them in order to find the elements that can be salvaged or adapted. If some parts of Neoclassicism, Marxism, and Institutionalism turn out to be useful and can be integrated into a new and more illuminating explanation, then this is what should be done. Such an approach is encouraged by Feminists.

VIEWS OF HUMAN NATURE AND JUSTICE

Feminist economists believe that *Homo sapiens* are social animals and that cultural factors are therefore important determinants of behavior. The inferior status of women, for example, is not a function of nature or objective processes, it is learned. It is impossible to understand the factors affecting economic wellbeing or to recommend policy if this is ignored. In terms of justice, Feminist economists argue that people of every gender and ethnicity should be free to make their own choices. That this is often prevented by legal and social factors means that, for Feminists, proposals must by necessity range well outside of traditional categories like monetary and fiscal policy. There is no other way to improve the lot of women and other disadvantaged groups. Empowering people is every bit as, if not more, important than lowering unemployment or inflation.

STANDARDS

Primary

One cannot really be a Feminist economist and believe that existing economic and social differentials between men and women are natural or objectively determined. Nor is it likely that rejecting the idea that power is an important consideration would be acceptable. Last, that economics is necessarily value-laden and that a key part of our undertaking is to recommend policy to better people's lives are both important elements of Feminism.

Secondary

All that said, the pluralistic and interdisciplinary nature of Feminist economics leaves the researcher with a great deal of latitude outside these primary standards. Their openness means that not only would works containing elements of Neoclassicism, Marxism, and Institutionalism be potentially acceptable, but also those drawing from sociology, political science, literature, and so on, and various strands therein. Popular research themes in Feminist economics include development, history, methodology, and non-market activities.

CONTEMPORARY ACTIVITIES

The primary group for Feminist and Gender economists is the International Association for Feminist Economics. Their web page (http://www.iaffe.org/) advertises a number of activities:

- Organization of an annual conference to present current research, plan future research, and interact with economists and advocates with similar interests.
- Organization of sessions at national, regional, and international meetings of economists.
- Publication of a newsletter that reports on activities, opportunities, and resources of interest.
- Maintenance of an electronic mail network to provide quick and low-cost communication among subscribers interested in Feminist economics.
- Compilation of bibliographies, course syllabi, and a list of working papers on Feminist economics.
- Publication of a scholarly journal, *Feminist Economics*, to increase awareness of Feminist research in economics.[2]

Feminist economics is a very active area and one will find papers and presentations outside journals and conferences that are self-consciously focused on gender issues.

CRITICISMS

Some of the work done by Feminists would no doubt be viewed as better suited to sociology or history, particularly by Neoclassical economists. It is not so much that it is not worthwhile, it is just not economics. In addition, mainstream economists generally view approaches that eschew complex mathematical modeling as soft, meaning that they lack the rigor and the reliability of "real" science. Feminist economics certainly falls under this category.

FINAL REJOINDER

The argument against ignoring non-market work in economics was already made above, but the gist of it is that if our discipline is about the determinants of the material wellbeing of humans, it makes no sense to ignore the contributions of a large percentage of *Homo sapiens* just because they did not sell their services. Not only do markets exist for many of these activities, but even if they were of no value in and of themselves – which is certainly not the case – they support our ability to carry out market transactions. Caring labor creates market labor. Even more troubling to Feminists is the idea that we should differentiate between market and non-market labor at all. This is, they say, again derivative of the masculinst bias in our culture and discipline.

Likewise, the view that abstract, rational math is somehow superior to other forms of modeling (pattern modeling, storytelling, history, case study, participant-observer, and so on). What tool we employ should be a function of what would best answer the question at hand, not what is viewed as the most difficult to master. The latter is a result of male competitiveness. In point of fact, say Feminists, a great deal of human behavior is too complex to reduce to a set of simultaneous equations so that when we force our studies into these restrictive and overly rigid formats we actually obscure rather than illuminate. Economists' obses- sion with advanced mathematics is a function of masculine posturing, not careful methodology.

FURTHER READING

There are a number of excellent collections and general guides. For example, *The Elgar Companion to Feminist Economics* (Peterson and Lewis 1999), while older, offers not only an encyclopedic treatment of the topic that is not limited to any particular school of thought, but vital references for each. *The Economics of the Family* (Folbre 1996) covers Neoclassical and Institutionalist contributions and both *Beyond Economic Man* (Ferber and Nelson 1993) and *Feminist Economics Today* (Ferber and Nelson 2003) are also useful collections. The journal *Feminist Economics* has many articles that are non-technical and accessible. Finally, although there are many Feminist blogs, only a few focus on economics, per se. *Lady Economist* (ladyeconomist.com) is probably the best and is quite active.

NOTES

1. This is not to say that child rearing and so on should be the exclusive domain of women. However, that is the case in many cultures and, at least for the time being, it is a reality that must be addressed.
2. The journal is open to work across the spectrum discussed in this chapter and was the winner of the Best New Journal award in 1997 from the Council of Editors of Learned Journals (http://www.celj.org/best_new_journal).

REFERENCES

Albelda, R. (1997), *Economics & Feminism: Disturbances in the Field*, New York: Twayne Publishers.

Barker, D.K. (2005), "Beyond women and economics: rereading 'women's work,'" *Signs*, **30** (4), 2189–209.

Becker, G.S. (1981), *A Treatise on the Family*, Cambridge, MA: Harvard University Press.

Becker, G.S. (1985), "Human capital, effort, and the sexual division of labor," *Journal of Labor Economics*, **3** (1), S33–S58.

Dugger, W. (1994), "Institutionalism and feminism," in J. Peterson and D. Brown (eds), *The Economic Status of Women Under Capitalism: Institutional Economics and Feminist Theory*, Aldershot, UK and Brookfield, VT, USA: Edward Elgar, pp. 3–18.

Ferber, M.A. and J.A. Nelson (1993), *Beyond Economic Man: Feminist Theory and Economics*, Chicago, IL: University of Chicago Press.

Ferber, M.A. and J.A. Nelson (2003), *Feminist Economics Today: Beyond Economic Man*, Chicago, IL: University of Chicago Press.

Figart, D.M. and E. Mutari (1999), "Feminist political economy: paradigms," in P.A. O'Hara (ed.), *Encyclopedia of Political Economy*, Cheltenham, UK and Northampton, MA, USA: Edward Elgar, pp. 335–7.

Folbre, N. (1996), *The Economics of the Family*, Cheltenham, UK and Brookfield, VT, USA: Edward Elgar.

Hartmann, H. (1981), "The unhappy marriage of Marxism and Feminism," in L. Sargent (ed.), *Women and Revolution: A Discussion of the Unhappy Marriage of Marxism and Feminism*, Boston, MA: South End Press, pp. 1–41.

Hewiston, G.J. (1999), *Feminist Economics: Interrogating the Masculinity of Rational Economic Man*, Cheltenham, UK and Northampton, MA, USA: Edward Elgar.

Hewitson, G.J. (2003), "Domestic labor and gender identity: are all women carers?," in D.K. Barker and E. Kuiper (eds), *Toward a Feminist Philosophy of Economics*, Cheltenham, UK and Northampton, MA, USA: Edward Elgar, pp. 266–83.

Hewitson, G.J. (2010), "Feminist economics," in R. Free (ed.), *21st Century Economics: A Reference Handbook*, Thousand Oaks, CA: Sage, pp. 901–13.

Howard, M.C. and J.E. King (1992), *A History of Marxian Economics: Volume II, 1829–1990*, Princeton, NJ: Princeton University Press.

Miller, E.S. (1972), "Veblen and women's lib: a parallel," *Journal of Economic Issues*, **6** (2/3), 75–86.

Nobel Foundation (n.d.), *The Sveriges Riksbank Prize in Economic Sciences in Memory of Alfred Nobel 1992*, available at http://nobelprize.org/nobel_prizes/economics/laureates/1992/ (accessed June 2, 2011).

Peterson, J. and M. Lewis (1999), *The Elgar Companion to Feminist Economics*, Cheltenham, UK and Northampton, MA, USA: Edward Elgar.

Veblen, T. (1898–99), "The barbarian status of women," *American Journal of Sociology*, **4**, 503–14.

Waddoups, J. and R. Tilman (1992), "Thorstein Veblen and the feminism of institutional economics," *International Review of Sociology*, **3** (2), 182–204.

10. Conclusions

I challenged you at the end of the first chapter to come away from this book without thinking that you found something interesting and insightful in every school of thought. By that, I did not mean that I expected you to become a Neoclassical-Marxist-Austrian-Post Keynesian-Institutionalist-New Institutionalist-Feminist economist, but that you would at some point in every chapter see a concept that made you stop and consider what you had just read. As for myself, I did that very thing many times as I did the research for this volume. I thought I was an open-minded, pluralistic economist before writing this, and I suppose I was compared to many. However, my conviction has been magnified several times over as I have not only learned more about each paradigm, but experienced the kind, enthusiastic, and thoughtful manner in which representatives of the various schools of thought have offered help and criticism. Today, I have an even greater sense of respect for them and their colleagues.

Mutual respect is a missing ingredient today, which is part of the reason why so many economists are not bothered to learn anything about alternative perspectives. And that ignorance then reinforces the dismissive attitude. This is unfortunate and something that self-respecting scientists should not do. This is an opinion shared by those in the pluralism movement. They believe that the economics discipline would benefit tremendously from a more open discussion and that that would lead to greater understanding and mutual respect. They argue that this is necessary not simply because it would be polite, but because science is not an inevitable march from ignorance to truth. As explained in Chapters 2 and 3, Neoclassicism did not emerge as the dominant school of thought after a spirited scholarly debate. We did not carefully sift through all the non-mainstream approaches and incorporate whatever was deemed helpful while dropping the rest. Rather, historical developments were responsible for putting Neoclassicism at the top of the food chain and institutional inertia and path dependence kept it there. It had not been "proven" that Marxism, Austrianism, Post Keynesianism, Institutionalism, New Institutionalism, and Feminism were inferior. In fact, no one even tried to find out.

Please note that this is not meant to imply that it is Neoclassicism that should be dismissed. Far from it, it has insights every bit as useful (and not) as the others. Rather, it is the almost complete ignorance of the alternatives that is being decried here. The situation would be equally bad if history had conspired to put Marxism, Austrianism, or Institutionalism on top. The problem is that it is intellectually unhealthy to learn only one language. You never know how else it could be done or what is unique about your own approach and you are condemned to thinking inside the box since you have no idea what lies outside it. As John Maynard Keynes wrote, "It is astonishing what foolish things one can temporarily believe if one thinks too long alone, particularly in economics (along with the other moral sciences), where it is often impossible to bring one's ideas to a conclusive test either formal or experimental" (Keynes 1936, pp. vii–viii).

Of course, your typical practicing economist cannot spend equal amounts of time studying each paradigm. She must at some level pick one because it is impossible to express a view except from a view point. You cannot do a study on the impact of the minimum wage law from the Neoclassical-Marxist-Austrian-Post Keynesian-Institutionalist-New Institutionalist-Feminist perspective. However, what is being suggested here is that our goal should be to practice (and teach) economics in a manner consistent with William G. Perry's last stage of learning: commitment (Perry 1970). He hypothesized that college students started their course of study as dualistic thinkers who believe that there is "right" and "wrong" and that the people at the front of the classroom are authorities who are going to tell them which is which. One of our jobs as professors is to challenge this preconception and lead them to understand that multiple, reasonable perspectives are possible ("multiplicity"). Ultimately, however, we want them to move to commitment, where they adopt a particular view to use as their guide, but only tentatively and always with the knowledge that "I could be wrong." We want them to become mature, skeptical thinkers who realize that knowledge does not increase by slowly moving from darkness to light. In reality, there are tentative steps forward, followed by retreats and changes in direction. Unfortunately, this is not how economics has been done.

On the plus side, the pluralism movement appears to be strong and growing. A watershed event was the French student protest in 2000 (http://www.paecon.net/PAEtexts/a-e-petition.htm). They made a plea for being taught approaches other than just Neoclassicism, which they feared was out of touch with how the real world worked. This was an unexpected spark and it ignited other student protests and led to the foundation of the Real World Economics Network (http://www. paecon. net; see in particular the link to history and documents at the bottom of the page). Today, the latter has over 20,000 subscribers and offers resources and publication outlets for those interested in seeing our discipline become more open. In addition, the *International Journal of Pluralism and Economics Education* was inaugurated in 2009. And an increasing number of universities appear to be developing courses along the lines of this book (although, to my knowledge, ours is the only economics department where such a class is required of all majors). So, even if we are still a long way from a pluralistic economics, it cannot be said that progress is not being made. It is my sincere hope that, after having read this book, you are now part of that movement as well.

One issue remains. I promised in Chapter 1 to conclude by telling which schools of thought I tend to follow: I was trained as a Neo-classical, but eventually found myself primarily in the Post Keynesian and Institutionalist camps. Now you know!

REFERENCES

Keynes, J.M. (1936), *The General Theory of Employment, Interest and Money*, London: Macmillan.
Perry, W.G. Jr (1970), *Forms of Intellectual and Ethical Development in the College Years: A Scheme*, New York: Holt, Rinehart, and Winston.

Index

Note: Due to the fact that this book is divided among seven different schools of thought, many topics are repeated. Though associations with specific paradigms are noted below when they are particularly significant, for the most part this was avoided in the interest of readability. However, for convenience of those searching for school of thought-specific information, the page spans for each are listed here:

a priori-ism 42
abstract reasoning 20, 42, 48, 52, 55, 102
action-axiom 77
aggregation
    Austrian objection to 77, 79, 81, 82
alienation 61, 70, 72, 73, 141
animal spirits 90, 95, 96, 97
anthropology 67, 70, 111, 121
apprenticeship of economists *see* training of economists
as-if method 47, 52, 55, 56, 102, 104, 129
Austrian business cycle theory 81–2
Austrian economics 1, 3, 5, 6, 29, 30, 34, 35, 43, 54, 55, 73, 76–87, 102, 124, 128, 129, 149, 150

banks
    central *see* monetary policy
    private 50, 51, 56, 64, 81, 85, 92, 93, 97, 104, 117, 127–8
Becker, Gary 138, 139
bourgeois 66, 68, 70, 72

business cycle 81–2, 83, 84, 85, 91, 94–6, 110
business firm 47, 48, 64, 67, 81, 82, 97, 116, 118, 124, 127

capital
    human 138, 139
    physical 44, 68, 77, 79, 81, 82, 91, 94, 96, 117
capitalism 2, 12, 27, 45, 59–74, 81, 85, 86, 89, 94, 97, 105, 106, 107, 110, 111, 118, 120, 122, 125, 126, 131, 140
cash 92, 93, 94, 102, 104, 106
catallactics 80
ceremonial 14, 21, 32, 110, 113, 114, 116, 117, 118, 121, 122, 141, 142
ceremonial-instrumental dichotomy 113–18
child 1, 8, 66, 135, 138, 139, 142, 143
class 10, 27, 60, 61, 62, 63, 65, 66, 67, 69, 70, 71, 73, 122, 140, 141, 142
classical economics 62–3
Coase, Ronald 132